Fostering Creativity and Innovation

Flevy Lasrado

Fostering Creativity and Innovation

Creating a Sustainable Innovation Environment in the United Arab Emirates

palgrave
macmillan

Flevy Lasrado
University of Wollongong in Dubai
Dubai, United Arab Emirates

ISBN 978-3-319-99120-7 ISBN 978-3-319-99121-4 (eBook)
https://doi.org/10.1007/978-3-319-99121-4

Library of Congress Control Number: 2018952660

This Palgrave Macmillan imprint is published by the registered company Springer Nature Switzerland AG
The registered company address is: Gewerbestrasse 11, 6330 Cham, Switzerland

Foreword

In 1996, *Business Week* ran a cover story predicting the demise of Apple with a headline "The Fall of an American Icon." Today, as I am writing this Foreword, Apple has become the first company to have a market capitalization of one trillion dollars. Innovation has been at the core of this phenomenal growth of Apple. However, Apple's story is not a standalone. Some of the world's most admired companies are also the most innovative companies. It is to this backdrop that Flevy Lasrado's book, *Fostering Creativity and Innovation: Creating a Sustainable Innovation Environment in the United Arab Emirates*, gains particular significance.

Lasrado presents a very lucid account of factors that make some organizations more innovative than others. The book has six chapters. In the first chapter, she starts with a general discussion about the importance of innovation and creativity and what they mean for global entrepreneurs. She then introduces the UAE as an innovation hub in Asia and discusses the importance of innovation for the UAE economy, and how the same has evolved over the years. Chapter 2 goes on to identify the factors that make some organizations more innovative than others. Lasrado emphasizes the role of organizational culture which helps bring forth the creativity of its employees. Using the ability, opportunity, and motivation framework, Lasrado encourages entrepreneurs to make their organizations more conducive for fostering an innovation culture.

In the formal organizational settings, managers need tools to assess performance outcomes so that corrective measures can be implemented. Chapter 3 discusses the assessment tools for evaluating an organization's level of creativity and innovation using the 4C framework. Lasrado presents several case studies to explain the four criteria of the assessment model—leadership, people, capability-building, and innovation outcomes. Chapter 4 focuses on tools to assist the organizations to evaluate their innovation initiatives and develop a plan of action for improving innovation performance. Building on the 4C framework presented in the previous chapter, Lasrado develops a Creativity and Innovation Assessment Maturity (CIAM) tool. The CIAM tool is quite versatile as it can help assess innovation from grassroots efforts to large-scale, world-class deployments. Using this tool, organizations can continuously challenge themselves to achieve a higher level of innovation performance.

Chapter 5 takes a more global perspective on innovation with a discussion of global standards and frameworks for assessing innovation. This is done with the help of various global innovation awards and what organizations need to do to compete for these awards. I find this chapter very hands-on as Lasrado challenges organizations to pursue specific initiatives rather than leaving things in vouge. She presents several case studies of both public and private sector organizations to demonstrate what it takes to be a high innovation organization. Finally, Lasrado discusses the challenges of sustainable innovation, which should be focused on the four key areas of profitability, sustainability, reputation, and governance. After all, the benefits from innovation can be realized only when organizations continue to pursue innovation in the long run in a sustainable manner. Lasrado also discusses several themes and presents propositions for advancing academic work in this domain.

All in all, this is a very interesting work, which should add value to both practitioners as well as academic readers. With just over 150 pages, it is easy reading material but will surely challenge many assumptions that managers hold about creativity and innovation in organizations.

Newark, NJ, USA
August 2, 2018

Ajai Gaur

Contents

1 **Building a Strong Foundation for a High-Functioning Culture of Creativity and Innovation** 1

1.1 Introduction to Organizational Creativity and Innovation 1

1.2 Challenges of Global Entrepreneurship for Innovation 7

1.3 Concepts of Design Thinking and Tools for Ideation 10

1.4 Shaping Innovation Deployment 13

1.5 Importance of Innovation in the United Arab Emirates 15

1.6 Innovation Legacy: The Case of the United Arab Emirates 21

1.7 Conclusion 25

References 28

2 **TQM, AMO, and Factors Impacting Organizational Creativity and Innovation** 35

2.1 Theoretical Underpinnings 35

2.2 Transition from Quality to Innovation 35

2.3 Bringing in Tools: What Can We Learn from Total Quality Management (TQM) to Innovate? 37

2.4 Power of Ability, Opportunity, and Motivation (AMO) 41

2.5 Conclusion 44

References 46

3 A Framework for Assessing Innovation 51
3.1 Introduction 51
3.2 Understanding Enablers and Outcomes 52
3.3 Component 1: Leadership 54
3.4 Component 2: People 61
3.5 Component 3: Capability-Building 65
3.6 Component 4: Innovation Outcomes 75
3.7 Preliminary Framework and Maturity Stages 78
3.8 Conclusion 81
References 83

4 "How Are We Doing?" Using a Maturity Model Assessment 89
4.1 Introduction 89
4.2 Maturity Model Assessment Structure 91
4.3 Creativity and Innovation Assessment Maturity (CIAM) Tool 94
4.4 How to Use the CIAM Tool 111
4.5 Measuring Progress and Success Using the CIAM Tool 117
4.6 Defining the Path to Success 120
4.7 Conclusion 125
References 126

5 Innovation in Action 127
5.1 Innovation Assessment and Awards 127
5.2 UAE Innovation Award 128
5.3 ASQ Innovation Award 131
5.4 Leading for Innovation: What It Is, What It Is Not—a Case of Dubai Quality Group 139
5.5 Innovation Profile of Ducab 148
5.6 Conclusion 156
References 156

6 Sustaining Innovation and Future Research Implications 157
6.1 Introduction 157
6.2 Lessons from Top Innovative Companies 158
6.3 Sustaining Innovation 162
6.4 A Theoretical Framework for the Sustainable Innovation Engine 168
6.5 Conclusion 181
References 182

Index 189

List of Figures

Fig. 2.1	The AMO framework and its linkages to the 4c model	44
Fig. 3.1	Innovation framework	53
Fig. 3.2	Maturity stages	81
Fig. 6.1	Sustainable innovation engine	169

List of Tables

Table 1.1	Most innovative companies of 2018	27
Table 3.1	The 4C framework of innovation assessment	79
Table 4.1	Scoresheet for leadership enabler	92
Table 4.2	Maturity table for leadership component	94
Table 4.3	Scoresheet for people component	101
Table 4.4	Maturity table for people component	102
Table 4.5	Scoresheet for capability building component	107
Table 4.6	Maturity table for organizational capability component	108
Table 4.7	Scoresheet for innovation outcomes	110
Table 4.8	Maturity table for innovation outcomes	111
Table 4.9	Assessment framework	112
Table 4.10	Maturity scores	117
Table 4.11	Example assessment	121
Table 5.1	UAE innovation award winners, 2017	130

1

Building a Strong Foundation for a High-Functioning Culture of Creativity and Innovation

1.1 Introduction to Organizational Creativity and Innovation

Innovation is a potent way to tackle some of the biggest problems in the world around us. In the business world, individual examples such as our opportunities for social interaction during product retail appear to have significant impact, enabling us to receive highly sophisticated services. Further, mobile phones and computers have transformed the speed, social code, and mediums used to communicate. Truly, the second decade of the twenty-first century has witnessed the rise of global competitiveness based on innovation advantage (National Research Council [NRC] 2012). In response, advanced and emerging nations are developing and pursuing innovation policies. Despite this recent interest, innovation started evolving as a key discipline of research during the twentieth century. In the knowledge economy, innovation is the most important source of change (Dajić 2017).

Innovation is crucial for the Gulf Cooperation Council (GCC) countries as it is for many regions, and innovation is no stranger to Middle

F. Lasrado, *Fostering Creativity and Innovation*,
https://doi.org/10.1007/978-3-319-99121-4_1

East Northern Africa (MENA) as the CEO of Shell noted recently in relation to the importance of energy innovation for the region (PR Newswire 2017).

Today, innovations are widely recognized not only as an engine of economic development and social progress (Randhawa and Scerri 2009) but also as an avenue for organizations to create value and competitive advantage (Pitelis 2009). High-performing organizations have their innovation belts under control and are able to successfully sustain the volatile momentum of market expansion, globalization, and technological advancement. As such, innovation offers organizations the highest potential for competitive advantage in the twenty-first century. Previously, quality, productivity, and access to low-cost resources were significant factors offering competitive advantage, but these factors are becoming less important in recent times.

Although innovation can influence organizational transformations, the field of innovation assessment is still insufficiently understood. Frameworks exist for its effective implementation in professional and public contexts, but assessment frameworks in organizational contexts are few. Innovation assessments can help managers and senior management lead a successful deployment of innovation across the organization. Effective implementation of innovation frameworks can significantly benefit organizations. For example, innovations have enhanced services and products and positively affect design processes for improved outputs. However, the success of innovation is concerned with how innovation design can shape or influence innovation levers for sustainable innovation. To understand this success fully, it is important to start our journey by understanding what innovation is.

The scope of innovation is vast with researchers offering various definitions of the term and their own visions of innovation-driving factors such as leadership and organizational capabilities. Moreover, innovation is complex, making it difficult to answer the question: "What is innovation?" Despite the dozens of possible definitions, it is crucial for an organization to understand innovation to drive this focus forward. So, we begin by asking: What does innovation mean to organizations?

Beginning with one of the oldest definitions, innovation is the generation, acceptance, and implementation of new ideas, processes, products, or services (Thompson 1965). Innovation occurs when value is created for the customer (Baunsgaard and Clegg 2009), and value creation is the process through which users become better off in some respect (Grönroos 2008). In other words, innovation must result in solving customers' problems, leading to a better customer experience.

While value creation is one aspect of innovation, other definitions have held that profit is central to innovation. In this sense, we acknowledge that ideas have to be prototyped and should result in new products and services that yield profit for the organization. Echoing the message of "newness" in innovation, Baunsgaard and Clegg (2009) defined innovation as the creation of novelty that provides economic value through the creation of new products and services. This "newness," as Keupp et al. (2012) noted, can relate to a "new product or service, a new production process technology, a new structure or administrative system, a new plan or program pertaining to organization members." We find such newness embedded in the products or services produced by the organization. We see newness in the mobile phones or banking services that we use today or the way we collaborate with others in an organization. The newness of these products results from the way innovation has transformed them. In this sense, we are not experiencing fundamentally new products or discoveries as they were in existence before. Still, we still see an enhanced or new product due to innovation. The whole idea of being able to transform to meet the needs and wants of global customers underpins innovation as opposed to discovery. Therefore, this newness can be achieved by changing the production process, making new plans, or forming administrative structures in an innovative way.

Over the past forty years, there have been numerous definitions created to capture the notion of innovation (Estelyiová and Žižlavský 2012). Despite nuanced differences, most definitions have highlighted new and profit-earning initiatives while others have hinted at social impacts as well. Entrepreneurial functions may occur not only within private businesses, but also in the community sector and public agencies. Further, as cited in

Ţîţu et al. (2015), the notion of "innovation" from the economic point of view was analyzed for the first time by the Austrian scientist J. Schumpeter in the first decade of the twentieth century. In his work *Theory of Economic Development*, Schumpeter defined innovation as "the totality of changes having as a purpose the implementation and usage of the new types of products, means of production and transport, outlet markets and forms of organization of the production process." In Schumpeter's framework, an innovation is recognized as being one of five types of activities, namely: (1) creating a new product, (2) introducing a new method of manufacture, (3) entering (or creating) a new outlet market, (4) using a new raw material, or (5) developing a new company structure. Along similar lines, the European Commission defined innovation as "the conversion of the new knowledge into economic and social benefits, as a result of the interaction between various subjects of a system that includes companies, research institutions and financiers in a local, national or international frame" (Ţîţu et al. 2015). Moreover, innovation can be understood as a process of learning and knowledge creation through which new problems are defined and new knowledge is developed to solve them (Lam 2010). It is defined as "the intentional generation, adoption and application of new processes, products or procedures that aim to benefit the individual, group or organization in question" (Lipponen et al. 2008). Summing this all up reveals that innovation is about the creation and implementation of a new idea in a social context with the purpose of delivering commercial benefits (Khairuzzaman et al. 2007).

When innovation is nurtured effectively, it can help an organization to outperform its competitors and can ensure sustainable growth. Specially, innovation is recognized as one of the five key drivers of firm-level productivity along with investment, skills, enterprise, and competition (Camus 2007).

In turn, innovation is driven by employees' resources: creativity, competence, and problem-solving abilities (Hoyrup 2010). So, the question arises: Which comes first, creativity or innovation? Before we explore this question, let us also define creativity. In an organization, creativity is a continuous search for, and solving of, problems and the creation and implementation of new solutions for the betterment of the organization, its customers, and its members (Baccarani 2009). Creativity is usually defined as the production of novel ideas that are useful and appropriate to the situation. Entrepreneurs clearly have an obligation in steering creative ideas into useful solutions. It is of vital importance to understand that creative ideas provide a firm the basis for innovation. An idea requires nurturing to spur innovation. Creativity has many synonyms, such as productive thinking, divergent thinking, originality, imagination, brainstorming, and so on (Chen and Kaufmann 2008). Oldham and Cummings (1996) defined creative performance as products or procedures that satisfy two conditions:

- they are novel or original, and
- they are potentially relevant or useful to an organization.

Creativity has been long described as proposing something new. While this remains true, it is also important that something that is newly proposed must also must be valuable or meet its purpose. This expectation implies that new ways to do something must create value. Definitions for the term *creativity* commonly describe novelty and usefulness as core dimensions.

Indeed, to spur creativity in an organization, one will have to condition one's thinking to understand the needs of the company as well as the end user's pain points. Creating an end user experience would help innovators to imagine all the perspectives of the pain points. This way of thinking is vital, as evidenced by the creativity exhibited by some companies today.

In today's competitive business world, both product-based and service-based innovations are gaining importance. While product-based innovations may largely depend on technical and professional capabilities, cultural or human-related capabilities are significant in service innovations. Creativity spurs such innovations in organizations.

Creativity alone does not guarantee success for the organization or lure the organization to be innovative. Innovativeness is harnessed when an organization arranges its creative thinking in an orderly manner and then puts a price on it or earns profits from it. Innovation success is about seeing an idea through to its fruition and gaining financial benefit from it. These endeavors in an organization have to be visible and deeply rooted for the firm to emerge as an innovative organization. Though creativity and innovation are often understood as synonymous or as two sides of a coin, they are different. An organization with a pool of ideas may not be able to emerge as innovative until those ideas have been put in practice and the organization has designed its products and services to be profitable.

Ideas (i.e. the creativity aspect) must be linked to innovation. Both aspects go hand in hand in defining the innovativeness of an organization. Employees indeed are sources of ideas, and the organization provides mechanisms such as structures and systems to convert them into profitable products or services. Because employees are a source of creative wealth, an organization must constantly foster this creativity in its employees and harness their creative ability to achieve sustainable business growth.

This focus on employee creativity takes us through the next several chapters of this book. Understanding these strong pillars that are to be adapted for an innovation drive is quite necessary for today's organizations to thrive. Organizations have to ensure that their business processes are clearly fostering activities along the line of the innovation belt just like various management approaches were adapted to cater to the changing dynamics of the business environment.

Moreover, innovative activities are embedded in employees' daily work activities—often in working teams—on the basis of their experience and on-the-job learning. Ideas can be generated anywhere, but innovation requires an organization whose knowledge, capabilities, and resources are being used to turn the idea into an innovation (Fagerberg 2005). So, the organization becomes central to the innovation as they leverage various resources for innovation and entrepreneurs, thereby becoming part of this innovation process (Cooley and Yorukogly 2003). As a result, entrepreneurs carry a responsibility to foster innovation. This gives us another perspective to understand innovation; specifically, Fagerberg (2005) stated that "innovations is by its nature a systematic phenomenon as it results from continuing interaction between different actors and organization." In short, we can conceptualize a product innovation as change occurring in what is offered and how these offerings are produced, implying a process innovation (Randhawa and Scerri 2008). Systematic diffusion of innovation is characterized by the spread and adoption of new ideas and knowledge (Cohen and Levinthal 1990). Randhawa and Scerri (2015) illustrated a five-stage process to understand how an innovation diffuses based on Mcguir (1989) and Prochaskas (1992):

- stage 1: Knowledge stage—comprehension of knowledge or skill for effective adoption of innovation;
- stage 2: Persuasion stage—contemplation on new behavior required for adoption of innovation;
- stage 3: Decision stage—preparation to try the innovation;
- stage 4: Implementation stage—action required for continued use of innovation; and
- stage 5: Confirmation stage—maintenance of the benefits resulting from the innovation through integration into ongoing routines.

This process of innovation can broadly be called closed innovation. Chesrough (2006) discussed the paradigm shift from closed to open innovation and noted that, in closed innovations, tight organizational control is required for innovation success as firms are responsible for creating, prototyping, and bringing them to the market themselves. Moreover, organizational innovation must also co-evolve with the environment (Baunsgaard and Clegg 2009). An open innovation is about allowing companies and a number of stakeholders to interact and co-create (Baunsgaard and Clegg 2009). In the next section, we will discuss the challenges facing global entrepreneurs when fostering innovation and the importance of putting organizational actors together along with co-evolving with the environment.

1.2 Challenges of Global Entrepreneurship for Innovation

It is a challenge for entrepreneurs to foster and sustain the creative wealth of the organization. What success factors are involved in steering the organization through this innovation era? Competitive ability is a top priority for entrepreneurs to survive in the twenty-first-century business context, which is characterized by organizational aspects such as diversity, gender balance, equity, and the ability to build on cultural competencies to achieve superior performance. Innovation should be regarded as an ongoing, everyday practice in organizations. Further, innovation and entrepreneurship are closely related, and the combination of the two is vital to organizational success and sustainability in today's dynamic and changing environment (Zhao 2005). What can global entrepreneurs do to maximize and coordinate their access to this diverse knowledge? We pay special attention to the challenges that entrepreneurs may encounter in developing, leveraging, and balancing their innovation arm.

Addressing the issue of rising to the challenges of innovation, Lasrado (2018) proposed several avenues for entrepreneurs to consider when fostering innovations, such as leadership, people, and organizational support. Going deep into this aspect, the author suggested good practices to leverage these innovations using questions such as those listed below.

1.2.1 Top Management Support

- How can I encourage the commitment to innovation at the top level of my organization?
- What examples can I cite of initiatives that fully support the innovation?
- Are employees supported enough?
- Do I feel a sense of cooperation among employees within the organization?
- Are we motivating employees to cooperate with their colleagues?

1.2.2 Organizational Support

- Am I proud of my innovation culture? If so, why?
- Is our creative ethos visible?
- How does our strategy cope with innovation needs?

- What are the communication formats that exist in our organization, and are they conducive enough to ignite innovation?

1.2.3 People

- Does our organization provide training to employees in relation to suggested schemes?
- What are these training programs?
- How would I describe the feedback system in our organization?
- Do employees receive support to resubmit their suggestions?

While this approach is of value, today's entrepreneurs face challenges from multiple dimensions. Internally, building innovation capabilities is one important element which requires a substantial investment in terms of resources. Externally, global entrepreneurs are required to co-evolve and co-create with various innovative environments. The aspects of crowdsourcing and crowdfunding offer huge opportunities, and entrepreneurs have to engage in them to derive a value for their firm. With a focus on managing the internal capability of the firm, we turn our attention to those capability-building aspects that are needed for entrepreneurs' attention and support. Although it is a challenge for managers or entrepreneurs to control the innovation journey, they can increase their odds of success by developing and practicing skills in learning, leading, relating, and cycling through the innovation journey (Van de Ven 2016).

Also, innovation does not have to be such an uncontrollable force; instead, it can be a rational management approach with its own distinct set of processes, practices, and tools (Bank and Raza 2014). Moreover, entrepreneurship and innovation are not confined to the initial stages of a new venture; rather, they are dynamic and holistic processes in entrepreneurial and innovative organizations. Organizational culture and management style are crucial factors affecting the development of entrepreneurial and innovation behavior in organizations calling for entrepreneurs' attention.

The entrepreneurial journey of transforming a business idea related to innovation into a feasible business is characterized by individual and collective uncertainties such as potential clients, investors, regulators, and other elements that comprise an innovation ecosystem (de Vasconcelos Gomes). As such, management of such critical elements becomes important for the innovation of organizations, especially radical innovations. Global innovative firms devise particular types of knowledge and capabilities that become embedded in the organization's culture (Knight and Cavusgil 2004). Global entrepreneurs therefore are required to develop and acquire innovations to better serve their customers.

Moreover, entrepreneurs support the process of funneling and implementing creative ideas that lead to an innovation. It is a known fact that sustaining innovation within organizations involves several coordination challenges that center on how innovation can be translated across space and time (Bartel and Garud 2009). In fact, creativity and innovation will occur only sporadically and will not thrive without a supportive environment and culture (Malaviya and Wadhwa 2005). Without doubt, the most innovative companies of the future will be dominated not by those that simply focus their energies on product and technical innovation but by those that have managed to build enduring environments of human capital striving toward innovation through the creation of appropriate cultures and climate. It is in this culture that leaders take responsibility to ensure various organizational elements come to play a role in facilitating the support within an organization toward an idea generation and steady innovations. The pool of creativity can then be developed for potential innovations. Enterprises and managers should consider promoting critical success factors such as leadership, top management support, organizational support, rewards, and evaluations to cultivate innovation. Entrepreneurs must know how to foster innovation and creativity in ways that help firms to create increasing amounts of wealth.

1.3 Concepts of Design Thinking and Tools for Ideation

Today's managers are seeking more creative problem-solving and lateral thinking in corporate innovation practices. In this section, we discuss how design thinking can be applied to assist in managing innovation. We first develop an understanding of the roots of design thinking and then discuss how some companies have deployed a design thinking approach.

Richard Buchanan was the first to link design thinking and innovation (Hautamäki and Oksanen 2015). Design thinking is mainly considered an American approach popularized by the design agency IDEO (Huhtamäki and Oksanen 2015). While design thinking has its roots in the 1960s, it grew in popularity during the 2000s (Ojasalo et al. 2015). What does this design thinking approach imply? Design thinking is a combined problem-centered and human-centered approach that draws stakeholders together; additionally, it is integrative, optimistic, and collaborative (Edwards et al. 2015). Unlike a straightforward and linear problem-solving process, a design thinking process focuses on continuous invention, learning, and experimentation and paying attention to idea generation and evaluation (Liedtka and Ogilvie 2011).

The approach is popular in innovation mainly because it brings empathic and participatory approaches and methods to deeply understand customers, their contexts, and latent needs (Ojasalo et al. 2015). As such, it is a discipline that uses the designer's sensibility and methods to match people's needs with what is technologically feasible and what a viable business strategy can convert into customer value and market opportunity (Brown and Katz 2009). It is about unwrapping the problem-solving process: It suggests that the creative process is not sequential, but overlapping and iterative; that it requires input from people from different disciplines and backgrounds; and that it is argumentative and requires integrative thinking (Edwards et al. 2015). Thus, design thinking offers a way to facilitate the open innovation processes that are needed to tackle wicked innovation challenges.

Because modern innovation processes involve foreseeing the future of an organization and finding partial solutions for problems regarding markets, customers, organizational culture, structure, and processes (Edwards et al. 2015), design thinking provides a good solution. Design thinking is a highly participatory, dialogue-based, and issue-driven approach, and its iterative nature aims at continuous invention and learning rather than stability and control (Shamiyeh 2010).

As previously mentioned, organizations face significant problems with innovation, which raises the question: How can an organization rise to innovation challenge? As innovation is a way forward, design thinking is a tool to smooth out this journey. Brown (2008) suggested that incorporating design thinking into all phases of the innovation process would offer a huge benefit. Design-driven innovators look for new ways to think about innovation, spend time with all kinds of consumers, and capture unexpected insights that more precisely reflect what people want (Hautamäki and Oksanen 2015).

Innovation also involves developing a strong ideation process, which is a crucial step in organizing a firm's innovation ability. While employees are expected to think creatively, the organization must put in place a system that enables employees to act on the needs of the ideation management. An ideation process can be visualized as employees organizing their thinking and putting forward a simple idea or a suggestion for the organization to act upon. For this ideation process to work, employees may need to connect with external or internal sources to fine tune their thinking while organizing and selecting their ideas for formal recognition.

Suggestion systems have been around for decades. Today, we see idea management systems within the organization that have paved the way for several of improvements and, in some cases, breakthrough innovation. An idea management system is an employee-involvement tool that organizations widely use to elicit employees' creative ideas. It is a means of facilitating the process of motivating employees to think more creatively, to share their creative thoughts, and to convert those ideas into valuable innovations. It also helps employees to think innovatively and creatively about their work and work environment and to produce ideas that will benefit the organization, for which the employee will receive recognition (Du Plessis et al. 2008). The roots of this system date back to 1721, when Yoshimune Tokugawa, the eighth shogun, placed a box called "Meyasubako" at the entrance of the Edo Castle for written ideas from his subjects. Although this is the most basic version of suggestion system known, the origin of an industrialized idea system can be traced back to the nineteenth century. In 1880, William Denny, a Scottish shipbuilder, asked his employees to offer ideas for better ways to build ships (Islam 2007). Following this, the Kodak company became a pioneer in this endeavor with its program introduced in 1896 (Carrier 1998). Thus, in the business world, formal and structured idea management systems were first introduced as a modern practice nearly one-hundred years ago. Such ideation tools are valuable, and organizations can enhance their ability to suit the needs of their individual setups by making use of them. A way forward is to consider the implementation of an idea management system as a source of innovation.

It is important to organize the process from idea extraction to idea follow-up properly; otherwise, employees will not be motivated to put their ideas forward (Van Dijk and Van den Ende 2002). Corporations that use idea management systems vary from small to large organizations and from private- to public-sector organizations. All organizations benefit from their idea systems, but the real success lies in the effectiveness of the implemented system. Van Dijk and Van den Ende (2002) noted that idea management systems can aim at different types of innovation, such as radical or incremental. It is possible for organizations to adapt their idea system depending on the environment in which they operate and the strategic choices that they make. Creativity is a basic human capability, and idea systems have the ability to capture creativity from the organization's employees.

Although innovation is more complicated than a box on the wall, enhancing such an ability could be the first step for start-ups. However, the box-on-the-wall approach can put the organization's innovation in limbo if an idea sits in the box for several weeks. Traditional methods can be revived for spontaneous actions, but employees in firms that want to be innovative must be given a mechanism and structure that allows them to capture their creative thinking.

1.4 Shaping Innovation Deployment

As we are living in a world that increasingly emphasizes knowledge application through the successful implementation of innovation (Ilić et al. 2004), research has suggested a direct link between performances, profit levels, and degrees of innovation (Bugnar et al. 2016). Hence, innovation has become a fundamental factor in the whole value chain (Bugnar et al. 2016). The new economy is greatly determined by the globalization process and frequent, radical changes, so innovations are crucial for organizations' growth and survival. In fact, the growing importance of innovation in achieving a sustainable competitive advantage resulted in a new concept for organizations (Ilić et al. 2014). Moreover, the term *innovation* describes not only a significant improvement in process and product technology, but also the innovation process in every sphere of human life, so communities, societies, and nations too have embraced it.

This spread of innovation has an enduring impact on organizations, organizations have to expand their quality, service, and customer-centricity competence base, and they need to go beyond "reliable" products and services to innovate industry-leading offerings because breakthrough product innovation will be an important competence for the future (Chakravarthy and Yau 2017). Ganotakis and Love (2012, p. 1) stressed the importance of innovation by declaring that "innovation is central to the survival and growth of firms, and ultimately to the health of the economies of which they are part."

As John Koot (2016) said, "You can't expect different results by doing things the same old way!" Indeed, innovating businesses are successful for many reasons. They can sustain better firm performance (Dittrich and Duysters 2007), create competitive advantage, engage in value creation (Deeds et al. 2000), encourage economic development (Schumpeter 1934), and most importantly attain economic and social success in today's globalized business world (Castaño et al. 2016). Because innovation is considered one the most significant factors to enhance competitiveness on both national and international markets (Capitanio et al. 2010), it is even more important for organizations to shape their innovation deployment in a timely manner.

Innovation results from a complex process that combines curiosity, creativity, rigorous scientific method, and a suitable institutional framework of interaction (Sener and Schepers 2017). To shape innovation deployment effectively, organizations should properly account for the interests of various stakeholders, suitably employ their capabilities, and systematically mitigate any uncertainties or risks. This calls for systemic frameworks that help organizations roll out a strong culture for innovation.

Moreover, while innovation is not a straightforward process with a beginning and an end, it should still happen in an organized manner with a degree of strategy (Ţîţu et al. 2015). Further, as Ilić et al. (2014) noted, change is not new, but the speed of change is increasing. As a result, innovation should evolve as a strategic objective and the optimization of organizational resources in accordance with the organization's strategy guides to shape up the deployment of innovation. Particularly, an organization must invest in its innovation ability and treat innovations as assets for organizations to compete and secure competitive advantage. The outputs of innovation depend on time, money, and how companies perform their daily tasks (Mazzarol and Reboud 2011).

Creating a culture of innovation is quite important for innovation success. Such a culture is fostered through high-end practices. Highly innovative firms have created a unique culture moving away from simple performance-based organizations to be lean, agile, and highly creative. Ashish Server, a speaker at the 2018 Ideas Arabia conference in the UAE, echoed a strong message to "avoid theatre but create a culture." Twenty-first-century organizations must make innovation a way of life, so it is important that innovation deployment is ingrained in the culture rather than creating spaces or silos that lack the appropriate culture for innovation.

1.5 Importance of Innovation in the United Arab Emirates

Today, innovations are not only a matter for companies but also for nations (Tellis et al. 2008). In fact, firm-level innovation on aggregate is seen as the driver for economic growth and prosperity at the regional and national levels. As a result, a number of systematic frameworks of innovation have emerged that focus on technological, institutional, infrastructure, and economic drivers that support diffusion of innovation to occur on a regional or a national scale (Malebra 2005). National systems of innovations involve collaboration within the network of institutions in both public and private sectors for the development, diffusion, and use of innovation (Freeman 1987). This element of innovation has undoubtedly become the necessary condition for the sustainable development of a country or nation (Nasiri et al. 2016). Although the US is a world leader in innovation capacity according to several rankings (NRC 2012), China, Russia, India, Germany, and Singapore are among many other nations that are formulating comprehensive strategies to improve their innovation capacity.

The UAE government's vision is to become one of the most innovative governments globally by 2021. Emphasizing the importance of the country's innovation agenda, UAE President His Highness (H.H.) Sheikh Khalifa bin Zayed Al Nahyan declared 2015 the Year of Innovation. In line with this directive, H.H. Sheikh Mohammed bin Rashid Al Maktoum, UAE Vice President, Prime Minister, and Ruler of Dubai, launched various initiatives to promote innovation, including the National Innovation Strategy, which focuses on seven sectors: renewable energy, transportation, education, health, technology, water, and space. Further, Mohammed bin Rashid Centre for Government Innovation was launched in September 2014 to encourage and motivate innovation in the public sector, as described in Section 1.3. According to government.ae (2018), the government has encouraged innovation in the UAE to achieve several goals, as described below:

- to implement a sustainable investment plan in the UAE's human capital;
- to drive economic development away from the oil sector;
- to enhance the UAE's global competitiveness; and
- to introduce corporate methodologies and a culture for innovation.

The UAE has rapidly embraced the culture of innovation, as evidenced by its 35th ranking in the 2017 Global Innovation Index, topping all Arab countries. This ranking marked a climb from the previous year's 41st position, cementing the UAE's status as one of the world's most innovative countries. In recent years, the UAE has made tremendous progress in the area of innovation to remain competitive against more developed nations on the domestic and international markets through several of its programs.

The UAE has played a major role in introducing innovations in most of its services, and it continues to do so. The country has introduced new innovation and talent-related agencies, research centers, and deliberative spaces for inter-firm collaboration. For example, Dubai is a hub for innovation and technology, housing the Museum of the Future, the world's first 3D-printed building, and free zones promoting innovation. One of Dubai's most impressive innovative centers is the Mohammed bin Rashid Centre for Government Innovation which was established in September 2014 to stimulate and enrich the culture of innovation within the government sector through the development of an integrated innovation framework. The Centre holds Ibtikar Talks that aim at supporting the government sector in achieving a radical and comprehensive transformation in its operating model, enhancing cooperation between government entities to integrate innovation efforts at the national level, and stimulating innovation in the National Innovation Strategy's key sectors. The Centre also works on developing the innovative capabilities of government employees through a cohesive framework of innovation tools to grow highly skilled government innovators. The Centre sporadically organizes Government Innovation Labs aimed at inspiring innovative ideas and finding effective solutions to the challenges that face government entities. The Centre also launched a diploma in government innovation, which was awarded to fifty-five executives from federal and local government departments. These individuals were part of the first group embarking on the one-year diploma program. The idea behind this program was to develop next-generation innovation leaders and to enhance innovation culture within each of the government entities.

The UAE has adopted its own measurement tools including the Abu Dhabi Innovation Index to monitor progress toward innovation. Using input and output indicator data from 188 countries' economies, the index focuses on the creation of new socio-economic value, which is the most relevant to policymakers. The UAE government has also taken several steps and initiatives to promote and encourage innovation, all corresponding with Vision 2021 and aiming to make the UAE among the best countries in the world. These will be discussed in the UAE innovation legacy in the next section. The UAE presents a highly instructive case study of an innovative region that has successfully rolled out an innovation agenda and is seeking to improve its competitiveness in global innovation rankings.

Although innovation is not generally the hallmark of public sector behavior (Head 2011), the reverse is true in the UAE. The public sector has enthusiastically engaged in innovations. Like many governments at the national and provincial levels, the UAE has developed "regional" innovation programs aimed at achieving economic, social, and environmental objectives (Head 2011). The UAE has created a new position titled "CEO of Innovation" for every government department. This step reflects the UAE's keen interest in investing in management and leadership in the field of innovation. Further, the UAE cabinet ministers designated 2015 as the Year of Innovation, aiming for the UAE to become a world leader of innovation.

The importance of innovation can be attributed to the birth of the National Innovation Strategy, which was first announced by His Highness Sheikh Mohammed bin Rashid Al Maktoum, Vice President and Prime Minister of the UAE, on October 19, 2014. In February 2018, the UAE government approved the National Strategy for Advanced Innovation. This version of the National Innovation Strategy notes a new phase enabling people to shift from focusing on vital sectors to the goals and outcomes in seven areas: exploration, future skills, quality of health, living and life, green power, transport, and harnessing technology to serve humankind.

In addition to positioning the UAE among the world's top leaders of innovation, the strategy aims to develop a type of thinking that encourages experimentation and taking well-thought-out risks to achieve the goals of UAE Centennial 2071. Further reiterating the importance of innovation, Sheikh Mohammed stated:

> This innovation strategy is a national priority for our program of development and progress. It is a primary tool to achieve Vision 2021 and an engine for the growth of distinctive skills and capabilities across the nation. We have always called for creativity in every field: this strategy is a concrete step to implement that vision. These initiatives around innovation will enhance quality of life in the UAE and take our economy to new horizons. We want our public and private sectors to explore new horizons to develop our economy. Innovation is our only way to build a great history of the UAE. The future will be for those who adopt innovation. (www.uaeinnovation.ae)

Another important initiative was the development of the Government Innovation framework, which is intended to help public sector employees study about innovation in government. It will help employees cultivate, adopt, and shape new ideas according to their own needs. Moreover, one of the key indicators set for Vision 2021 have placed targets for 2021 that include to improve UAE ranking in the Global Innovation Index (www.uaeinnovation.ae).

Within organizations, "innovation weeks" have emerged to recognize the importance of employees' creative abilities. Breaking away from routine jobs and engaging in brainstorming sessions and dedicated activities are becoming work norms in many organizations. No industry is immune to innovation as it generates necessary competitive advantage that organizations will have to build on. A forward-thinking organization views employees as creative minds rather than simply heads on the payroll.

Moreover, a study by Alfantookh and Bakry (2015) suggested that the GCC countries are concerned with activating knowledge and innovation as a source of development that reduces their dependence on oil. The key message of UAE leaders is that "we must get our hands dirty and innovate, or accept stagnation." In addition, the UAE has established several innovation awards. For example, the Mohammed bin Rashid Al Maktoum Business Innovation Award gives businesses in the GCC something to strive for in terms of their innovation and business practices. The Umm Al Quwain Innovation Award was created to enhance the level of competition between various parties, including individuals, departments, government entities, and companies. Additional aims for the award are to create diversity in the knowledge-based economy, promote promising innovative practices, develop a culture of innovation in institutional work environments, and improve the quality of life. In 2015, another award was created to promote both creativity and innovation. This award, known as the Ministry of Interior Award for Innovative Policing Ideas, focuses on supporting policing services and organizing a conference that will be held every two years and include all the international police and security entities in the world.

In the UAE, innovation is the domain of not only commercial businesses, but also the public sector, the private sector, and the household sector. A study conducted by the Mohammed bin Rashid Centre for Government Innovation with the Massachusetts Institute of Technology (MIT) to measure household innovators in the UAE reported around 5% household-level innovation occurring in the UAE. In addition to inspiring innovation, the Mohammed bin Rashid Centre for Government Innovation has worked to compile a database that individuals and organizations can consult to find innovative experiences. The Centre hopes that this database will help establish a culture of innovation in the UAE community. The local innovation opportunities fall into one of five categories:

- A Service Innovation aims to offer new or improved services and create innovative ways to provide services.
- A Process Innovation is intended to develop innovative administrative and regulatory processes that will enhance institutional work.
- A Technology Innovation is one that looks for innovative, scientific solutions to the community's challenges and the development of advanced scientific facilities.
- A Policy Innovation results in the development of policies that will help create an environment that promotes innovation, progress, and development.
- A System Innovation will facilitate the creation of innovative systems that lead to innovative responses to challenges.

As Wentling (2015) observed, the UAE is no stranger to international attention for record-breaking achievements, but the sticking point this time will be maintaining the momentum to ensure an innovative culture reverberates for generations to come. In addition, a well-established seven-stage national innovation framework for government innovation further provides detailed guidance and tools to embark on innovation. Most innovations take place in the government sector, and their services have been well enhanced. This legacy is also rolling out in the private sector as the UAE's innovation awards are directed toward private-sector innovations. Indeed, it is necessary to develop a country-specific innovation model and strategies based on it in order to develop innovation. As with many organizations, the government of the UAE has begun to concentrate on government innovation by providing tools through the Mohammed bin Rashid Centre for Government Innovation. The Centre's tools and techniques are aimed at promoting initiatives and innovative solutions by government units to improve government sector efficiency while serving its clients. Examples of these tools are as follows:

- the Future Vision Board is intended to motivate and inspire;
- the Intelligence Game can help determine the participants' intelligence levels;
- the Building Block/The Hanger is a tool to develop innovative ideas and present them to others; and
- Challenges/Initiatives in Words can help the process of creative thinking.

Organizations looking to employ successful innovation management can look to research for numerous tools.

1.6 Innovation Legacy: The Case of the United Arab Emirates

As previously mentioned, the UAE is ranked 35th on the 2017 Global Innovation Index. In fact, it has climbed six places from the previous year's 41st position, strengthening its status as one of the world's most innovative countries and topping all Arab countries. Indeed, innovation is an important aspect of the "United in Knowledge" pillar of Vision 2021. It emphasizes the innovative *Emiratis* building a competitive economy. In accordance with Vision 2021, the UAE has taken several initiatives to inspire innovation, including the development of the Mohammed bin Rashid Centre for Government Innovation and its activities as described in the previous section. The UAE has also established two national strategies, the National Innovation Strategy (2014) and the National Strategy for Advanced Innovation (2018), both of which are described in more detail in Section 1.5. The UAE's legacy of innovation has further witnessed a celebration of 2015 as the Year of Innovation as the country has worked to create an environment that nurtures innovation.

Similarly, the UAE's Innovation Week in 2015 and innovation months in 2016 further introduced a widespread culture of innovation in the UAE. Further, the government has introduced an Emirates Science, Technology and Innovation Higher Policy that includes one hundred national initiatives with an investment budget of over $81.6 billion. The policy works toward establishing a solid future for the upcoming generation, moving away from the oil sector and creating a sustainable economy that will depend on science, knowledge, and technology. It will include special fields such as space research, specialized aviation industries, global pharmaceutical industries, solar power, civilian nuclear energy programs, robotics, and others.

In November 2015, the UAE launched a fund to finance innovation with a value of AED 2 billion. This is a federal initiative designed to provide financing solutions for innovators across various sectors in the UAE. Innovators can be individuals and companies registered in the country, and an innovation could be an idea, a technique, a process, a product, or a service. Priority will go to renewable energy, transport, education, health, technology, water, and space sectors, and applicants must provide a business development plan to be eligible for funding.

Another federal-level initiative known as Afkari was launched to support and fund innovative ideas of federal government employees that will contribute to the development of government services in the ministries and entities. Similarly, the Dubai Future Accelerators group is an initiative to enable rapid deployment of transformative technologies. The accelerators are programs and integrated systems designed to help entrepreneurs and innovators turn their ideas into successful companies. The purpose of this initiative is to bring together top international companies and entrepreneurs to address seven key twenty-first-century opportunities including:

- the application of cutting-edge technologies like artificial intelligence and robotics;
- genomics;
- 3D printing;

- biotechnology, and;
- new business models and best practices.

Another notable initiative is Dubai's focus on being a hub for innovation and technology with the Museum of the Future, which will become a unique incubator for futuristic innovations and designs and a major tourist destination. The Museum of the Future is expected to offer a platform to demonstrate and test the latest inventions and prototypes from up-and-coming start-ups and the world's technology giants. It will host innovation facilities and design studios with universities, companies, and research partners. It will also offer advanced courses and specialized workshops, as well as public talks and events.

Finally, the UAE's innovation legacy also boasts several innovation events and awards. One such event is the UAE Hackathon—Data for Happiness. The first hackathon aimed to use data to develop innovative solutions and ideas that contribute to the happiness of the community. It also aimed to engage a significant number of students with participants from other sectors of the society to develop modern solutions based on the analysis of available data. The UAE Hackathon will be an annual event revolving around several challenges, which include:

- transportation and traffic congestion;
- health and safety;
- sustainable development (post-oil age);
- environment and climate change;
- education;
- gender balance;
- enhancement of social relations in the UAE community, and;
- enhancement of lifestyle.

The UAE hosted the biggest innovation conferences. The conference took place in Dubai and offered a perfect platform for technological innovations and a chance for attendees to explore the role of innovation in a knowledge-based economy. There are several awards being established such as the Mohammed Bin Rashid Al Maktoum

Business Innovation Award, the Umm Al Quwain Innovation Award, and the Ministry of Interior Award for Innovative Policing Ideas, as discussed in the previous section. Similarly, the GovTech Prize is organized annually by the World Government Summit in Dubai to acknowledge pioneers and innovators in government technology for providing global solutions to global key challenges using blockchain technologies and strategies. In 2012, the International Award for the Arab Youth was established to support the Arab community's inventive young minds by catalyzing their creativity, excellence, and innovation, while building serious competition and expressing appreciation for their contributions and talent.

Finally, the UAE's key achievements in innovation are as below (see www.uaeinnovation.ae for more information):

- developing education and introducing computers and smart devices in schools;
- expanding the creation of higher education institutions;
- establishing a number of complexes, research institutions, and technical institutes to promote research, creativity, and innovation, such as:
  - Abu Dhabi's Masdar City
  - Dubai Science Park
  - Mohammed bin Rashid Solar Park
  - Arab Institution for Science and Technology in Sharjah
  - Technology and Innovation Center in Ras Al Khaimah, and
  - The Centre of Excellence for Applied Research & Training (CERT)
- spreading and providing information and communications technology to the public;
- encouraging the culture of eLearning in the governmental and non-governmental sectors;
- forming the Supreme Committee of UAE Innovation from a number of federal agencies, and;
- executing a Collaborative Care Agreement between the Ministry of Presidential Affairs and the Telecommunications Regulatory Authority

within the Be'tha scholarship program to provide the opportunity to study at the best international universities in specializations that serve the information and communications sector.

The following links are useful for reading more about UAE innovation:

- UAE Innovates—the UAE innovation website https://www.uaeinnovates.gov.ae/home
- Government Innovation—Ministry of Cabinet Affairs and Future—https://www.mocaf.gov.ae/en/area-of-focus/government-innovation
- National Innovation Strategy (2014)
- National Strategy for Advanced Innovation (2018)
- Science, Technology & Innovation Policy (PDF, 1.8 MB)—Ministry of Cabinet Affairs and Future
- Mohammed bin Rashid Innovation Fund—Ministry of Finance

1.7 Conclusion

Over the last decades, innovation has undoubtedly become increasingly recognized as a strategy for enabling a firm's competitive advantage. Despite this, we are still far from understanding its implementation and timely assessment to take full advantage of its benefits, especially through a systematic innovation assessment. The idea behind organizational innovation is to fulfil an unmet need and provide a new solution to a problematic situation. While it is important for this activity to be profitable for the organization, innovation may also result in social impacts. Given that the twenty-first-century economy is mainly characterized by the intensive use of knowledge, rapid changes, and hyper-competition, innovation is the factor that runs the new economy (Ilić et al. 2014). Today, the ability to innovate is one of the most important factors for creating competitive advantages and ensuring the success of any enterprise. Innovation is necessary for the survival, growth, and development of companies and for enhancing the company's competitive position (Petkovska 2015). On the whole, alongside thinking of innovation as new service, product, or technology, we can expand this vision to include imagining, mobilizing, and competing in new ways (Mootee 2013). Finally, getting onto the world stage as an innovator is commendable, but staying on it as an innovative global leader requires an organization to address transformation challenges. Global entrepreneurs therefore find ways to transform their companies for sustainable innovation management by fostering innovation leveraging factors.

Governments indeed have roles to play to spur innovation, and an empirical study suggested that the government should provide a conducive and enabling environment for these organizations by supplying them with basic amenities and infrastructure that will support their operation and enhance high productivity (Adebisi and Babatunde 2011). Most innovations fail, and an enterprise that does not innovate dies (Estelyiová and Žižlavský 2012).

In conclusion, the imperatives for innovation are growing stronger in both the government and the private sector of the UAE. The government has developed a coherent approach that should also be adopted by private organizations, which should assess their innovation initiatives through assessment programs. This usually means either developing internal methods, adopting frameworks, or even participating in external innovation-related award assessments. Overall, the aim of innovation should be both to increase value creation and to generate social impacts by balancing between service- and product-related innovations. After all, innovation occurs when we see the possibilities and opportunities that others are missing (Moustafellos 2015). Going forward, there is a need to include design knowledge in government policy that could contribute to the greater effectiveness of innovation initiatives. Building a strong foundation for innovation culture should, therefore, draw on sound frameworks that create a deep-rooted culture for innovation and a mind-set that embraces these approaches.

According to Boston Consulting Group (2018), the top fifty most innovative countries in the world (see Table 1.1) have in common their

Table 1.1 Most innovative companies of 2018

1	Apple	11	Airbnb	21	Siemens	31	Intel	41	3M
2	Google	12	SpaceX	22	Unilever	32	NTT DoCoMo	42	SAP
3	Microsoft	13	Netflix	23	BASF	33	Daimelr3	43	DuPont
4	Amazon	14	Tencent	24	Expedia	34	Axa	44	InterContinental Hotels Group
5	Samsung	15	Hewlett-Packard	25	Johnson and Johnson	35	Adidas	45	Disney
6	Tesia	16	Cisco systems	26	JPMorgan Chase	36	BMW	46	Huawei
7	Facebook	17	Toyota	27	Bayer	37	Nissan	47	Procter & Gamble
8	IBM	18	General Eclectic	28	Dow Chemical	38	Pftzer	48	Verizon
9	Uber	19	Orange	29	AT&T	39	Times Warner	49	Philips
10	Alibaba	20	Marriot	30	Allianz	40	Renault	50	Nestle

Source: 2017 BGC global innovation survey

ability to adopt technology. The report further stated that companies use data analytics for a variety of purposes connected with innovation, including identifying new areas for exploration, providing input for idea generation, revealing market trends, informing innovation investment decisions, and setting portfolio priorities. Moreover, organizations from sectors such as energy, media and entertainment, and financial services, including those in the public sector, have witnessed huge increases in terms of the number of organizations pursuing big data in innovation.

The focus of organizations should not be on incremental improvements but on exponential improvements. Organizations should develop a culture that constantly creates and problem-solves by adding new value through digitization. In this sense, it is imperative to ask: Do we have disruptive potential as an organization and hold a strong innovator mentality? Are we producing strong innovators? How likely is the organization to fail? If the organization does not fail, does it learn? Are we embedding learning from failure in our organization's culture? The Boston Group rankings of the world's top fifty innovative companies identified those with a highly innovative culture that exhibits not only a disruptive mentality but also a fail-forward mentality. Essentially, organizations should focus on speed, scale, and value elements to kickstart the innovation journey. Multiple methods such as design thinking, Lean Six Sigma, TRIZ, or agile tools can help progress the innovation culture. In the words of Ashish Server, an innovation practitioner who spoke at 13 Ideas Arabia, organizations should avoid the theater and build the culture. This directive is essential to building a strong foundation for innovation.

References

Adebisi, S.A., and B.O. Babatunde. 2011. Innovation Management and Organization Development in the Nigerian Banking System. *Bulletin* 63 (1): 1–82.

Alfantookh, A., and S.H. Bakry. 2015. Investigation of the State of Innovation in the Gulf Cooperation Council Countries: Looking Ahead. *Computers in Human Behavior* 48: 626–636.

Baccarani, C. 2009. What Do You Think Creativity Is and Where Can You Find It? *The Asian Journal of Quality* 6 (22): 91–101.

Bank, J., and A. Raza. 2014. Collaborative Idea Management: A Driver of Continuous Innovation. *Technology Innovation Management Review* 4 (2): 11.

Bartel, C., and R. Garud. 2009. The Role of Narratives in Sustaining Organizational Innovation. *Organization Science* 20 (1): 107–117.

Brown, T. 2008. Design Thinking. *Harvard Business Review* 86 (6): 84–92.

Brown, T., and B. Katz. 2009. *Change by Design: How Design Thinking Transforms Organisations and Inspires Innovation*. New York: HarperCollins.

Bugnar, N., L. Mester, and A. Fora. 2016. Innovation and International Competitiveness of a Country. *Annals of the University of Oradea., Economics Science Series* 25 (2): 35–43.

Camus, D., ed. 2007. *The ONS Productivity Handbook: A Statistical Overview and Guide*. Basingstoke: Office of National Statistics.

Capitanio, F., A. Coppola, and S. Pascucci. 2010. Product and Process Innovation in the Italian Food Industry. *Agribusiness* 26 (4): 503–518.

Carrier, C. 1998. Employee Creativity and Suggestion Systems Programs: An Empirical Study. *Creativity and Innovation Management* 7 (2): 62–72.

Castaño, M.S., M.T. Méndez, and M.Á. Galindo. 2016. Innovation, Internationalization and Business-Growth Expectations Among Entrepreneurs in the Services Sector. *Journal of Business Research* 69 (5): 1690–1695.

Chakravarthy, B., and D. Yau. 2017. Becoming Global Leaders: Innovation Challenges for Five Large Chinese Firms. *Strategy & Leadership* 45 (2): 19–24.

Chen, M.H., and G. Kaufmann. 2008. Employee Creativity and R&D: A Critical Review. *Creativity and Innovation Management* 17 (1): 71–76.

Chesbrough, H., ed. 2011. *Open Services Innovation: Rethinking Your Business to Grow and Compete in a New Era*. New York: Wiley.

Cohen, W., and D. Levinthal. 1990. Absorptive Capacity: A New Perspective on Learning and Innovation. *Administrative Science Quarterly* 35: 123–133.

Cooley, F.T., and M. Yorukogly. 2003. Innovation and Imitation in an Information Age. *Journal of the European Economic Association* 1 (2–3): 406–418.

Dajić, M. 2017. Role and Importance of Innovation in the Development of Serbian Economy. *Ekonomski signali: poslovni magazin* 12 (1): 55–64.

de Vasconcelos Gomes, L.A., M.S. Salerno, R. Phaal, and D.R. Probert. 2017. How Entrepreneurs Manage Collective Uncertainties in Innovation Ecosystems. *Technological Forecasting and Social Change*.

Deeds, D.L., D. DeCarolis, and J. Coombs. 2000. Dynamic Capabilities and New Product Development in High Technology Ventures: An Empirical Analysis of New Biotechnology Firms. *Journal of Business Venturing* 15 (3): 211–229.

Dittrich, K., and G. Duysters. 2007. Networking as a Means to Strategy Change: The Case of Open Innovation in Mobile Telephony. *Journal of Product Innovation Management* 24 (6): 510–521.

Du Plessis, A.J., A.E. Marx, and G. Wilson. 2008. Generating Ideas and Managing Suggestion Systems in Organisations: Some Empirical Evidence. *International Journal of Knowledge, Culture and Change Management* 8 (4): 133–140.

Edwards, M., D. Logue, and J. Schweitzer. 2015. Towards an Understanding of Open Innovation in Services: Beyond the Firm and Towards Relational Co-Creation. In *The Handbook of Service Innovation*, ed. R. Agarwal, W. Selen, G. Roos, and R. Green, 75–90. London: Springer.

Estelyiová, K., and O. Žižlavský. 2012. Boosting Innovation Through Interfirm-Cooperation. *Economics and Management* 17 (4): 1564–1571.

Fagerberg, J. 2005. Innovation: A Guide to the Literature. In *The Oxford Handbook of Innovation*, ed. J. Fagerberg, D.C. Mowery, and R.R. Nelson, 1–28. Oxford: Oxford University Press.

Freeman, C., ed. 1987. *Technology, Policy and Economic Performance: Lessons from Japan*. London: Pinter.

Ganotakis, P., and J.H. Love. 2012. Export Propensity, Export Intensity and Firm Performance: The Role of the Entrepreneurial Founding Team. *Journal of International Business Studies* 43 (8): 693–718.

Grönroos, C. 2008. Service Logic Revisited: Who Creates Value? And Who Co-creates? *EUR Business Research* 20 (4): 298–314.

Hautamäki, A., and K. Oksanen. 2015. Systemic Development of Service Innovation. In *The Handbook of Service Innovation*, ed. R. Agarwal, W. Selen, G. Roos, and R. Green. London: Springer.

Head, B.W. 2011. Governance for Sustainable Regions: Can Government Meet the Innovation Policy Challenge? *Regional Science Policy & Practice* 3 (3): 219–230.

Hoyrup, S. 2010. Employee-Driven Innovation and Workplace Learning: Basic Concepts, Approaches and Themes. *Transfer: European Review of Labour and Research* 16 (2): 143–154.

Ilić, D., S. Ostojić, and N. Damnjanović. 2014. The Importance of Marketing Innovation in New Economy. *Singidunum Journal of Applied Sciences* 11 (1): 34–42.

Islam, R. 2007. Evaluation of Suggestions by the Analytic Hierarchy Process: A Case Study on a Public University in Malaysia. viña del mar, Chile, August.

Keupp, M.M., M. Palmie, and O. Gassman. 2012. The Strategic Management of Innovation: A Systematic Review and Paths for Future Research. *International Journal of Management Reviews* 14 (4): 367–390.

Khairuzzaman, W., W. Ismail, and R. Abdmajid. 2007. Framework of the Culture of Innovation: A Revisit. *Jurnal Kemanusiaan* 9: 38–49.

Knight, G., and S.J. Cavusgil. 2004. *International Business Studies* 35: 124. https://doi.org/10.1057/palgrave.jibs.8400071.

Koot, J. 2016. Business: Innovation: The Importance of Innovation. *AJP: The Australian Journal of Pharmacy* 97 (1154): 59.

Lam, A. 2010. Organizational Innovation to Improve the Efficiency of Health Care Markets. *National Bureau of Economic Research Bulletin on Aging and Health* 2: 1–2.

Lasrado, F. 2018. Critical Success Factors of Innovation and Creativity for Global Entrepreneurs. In *Global Entrepreneurship and New Venture Creation in the Sharing Economy*, 75–91. Hershey: IGI Global.

Liedtka, J., and T. Ogilvie. 2011. *Designing for Growth: A Design Thinking Toolkit for Managers*. New York: Columbia University Press.

Lipponen, J., A. Bardi, and J. Haapamäki. 2008. The Interaction Between Values and Organizational Identification in Predicting Suggestion-Making at Work. *Journal of Occupational and Organizational Psychology* 81 (2): 241–248.

Malaviya, P., and S. Wadhwa. 2005. Innovation Management in Organizational Context: An Empirical Study. *Global Journal of Flexible Systems Management* 6 (2): 1–14.

Mazzarol, T., and S. Reboud, eds. 2011. *Strategic Innovation in Small Firms: An International Analysis of Innovation and Strategic Decision Making in Small to Medium Sized Enterprises*. Cheltenham: Edward Elgar.

Mootee, I. 2013. *Design Thinking for Strategic Innovation: What They Can't Teach You at Business or Design School*. Hoboken: Wiley.

Moustafellos, J. 2015. The Architecture of Service Innovation. In *The Handbook of Service Innovation*, ed. R. Agarwal, W. Selen, G. Roos, and R. Green. London: Springer.

Nasiri, A., A.R. Alleyne, and L. Yihui. 2016. Analysis of Innovation Management in German Enterprises. *Cogent Business & Management* 3 (1): 1216727.

National Research Council. 2012. *Rising to the Challenge: US Innovation Policy for the Global Economy*. Washington, DC: National Academies Press.

Ojasalo, K., M. Koskelo, and A.K. Nousiainen. 2015. Foresight and Service Design Boosting Dynamic Capabilities in Service Innovation. In *The Handbook of Service Innovation*, ed. R. Agarwal, W. Selen, G. Roos, and R. Green, 193–212. London: Springer.

Oldham, G.R., and A. Cummings. 1996. Employee Creativity: Personal and Contextual Factors at Work. *Academy of Management Journal* 39 (3): 607–634.

Petkovska, T. 2015. The Role and Importance of Innovation in Business of Small and Medium Enterprises. *Economic Development/Ekonomiski Razvoj* 17: 55–74.

Pitelis, C.N. 2009. The Co-evolution of Organizational Value Capture, Value Creation and Sustainable Advantage. *Organization Studies* 30 (10): 1115–1139.

PR Newswire. 2017. Shell Highlights Importance of Innovation and Technology in Today's World. *PR Newswire US*, March 6.

Randhawa, K., and M. Scerri. 2015. Service Innovation: A Review of the Literature. In *The Handbook of Service Innovation*, ed. R. Agarwal, W. Selen, G. Roos, and R. Green. London: Springer.

Sener, S., and S. Schepers, eds. 2017. *Innovation, Governance and Entrepreneurship: How Do They Evolve in Middle Income Countries?* doi:https://doi.org/10.1007/978-3-319-55,926-1_1

Shamiyeh, M., ed. 2010. *Creating Desired Futures: How Design Thinking Innovates Business*. Basel: Walter de Gruyter.

Tellis, G.J., A.B. Eisingerich, R.K. Chandy, and J.C. Prabhu. 2008. Competing for the Future: Patterns in the Global Location of R&D Centers by the World's Largest Firms. *ISBM Report* 6.

Thompson, D.L. 1965. Survey Data as Evidence in Trademark Infringement Cases. *Journal of Marketing Research* 64–73.

Ţîţu, A.M., A.S. Răulea, and S. Ţîţu. 2015. Innovation: A Challenge for the 21st Century Managers. *Procedia Economics and Finance* 27: 126–135.

Van Dijk, C., and J. Van den Ende. 2002. Suggestion System: Transferring Employee Creativity into Practicable Ideas. *R&D Management* 32 (5): 387–395.

Wentling, E. 2015. Innovation, Not Oil, Key to Future of UAE. *The Telegraph*. http://www.telegraph.co.uk/sponsored/united-arab-emirates/12026654/Innovation-not-oil-key-to-future-of-UAE.html

Zhao, F. 2005. Exploring the Synergy Between Entrepreneurship and Innovation. *International Journal of Entrepreneurial Behavior & Research* 11 (1): 25–41.

2

TQM, AMO, and Factors Impacting Organizational Creativity and Innovation

2.1 Theoretical Underpinnings

Fostering innovation in an organization has several theoretical roots. We will first attempt to understand the theoretical underpinnings that can support the four components of the innovation assessment framework discussed in Chap. 3. The four enablers are leadership, people, dynamic organizational capability, and innovation outcomes. While the three core components embrace broad theories of management, our focus in this chapter is to illustrate the ability, opportunity, and motivation (AMO) framework and total quality management (TQM) in particular. In light of these, the assessment framework can help to foster good practices to elevate an organization's innovation status. The concluding Chap. 6 further draws on several useful theories to discuss a theoretical framework for sustaining an innovation engine.

2.2 Transition from Quality to Innovation

Today's business environment features a change in priority from quality to innovation. In many business sectors, the focus on quality management as a competitive strategy is being replaced by a focus on innovation

F. Lasrado, *Fostering Creativity and Innovation*,
https://doi.org/10.1007/978-3-319-99121-4_2

(Leavengood et al. 2014). To stay on par with the latest technology and competitive environments, companies are looking to improve their innovation skills. The literature has discussed numerous companies that have benefited from innovation and increased their profits and market share (Zehir et al. 2012). In fact, it has become quite a challenge to integrate both quality and innovation into organizations.

When drive by innovation, leaders do not create followers; rather, they create leaders who can think, act, and implement their ideas independently. Indeed, this is not so different from the teaching of quality philosophers. Among Deming's fourteen points for quality, one key element was institute leadership. While quality is important, innovation is the next big step.

We are witnessing an era in which customers ascertain the future of any company. While a focus on such customers is at the heart of quality systems, the transition to innovation is a natural way to meet customer needs in a new manner. To achieve and improve quality, innovation plays a major role by identifying new pathways to inventions and discoveries. Learning is understood to be an important intermediary between quality and innovation, but care must be taken to ensure that innovative ideas go hand-in-hand with quality requirements to maintain standards.

O'Neill et al. (2016) uncovered the roots of quality management underlying Deming's theory. They explained that, according to Deming's theory, quality management helps to improve the factors that can enhance the performance of the organization. For example, if an organization has the ability to learn for the betterment of product quality, the organization has the ability to improve performance that will result in product quality improvement. Doeleman et al. (2014) stated that this European Foundation for Quality Management (EFQM) framework is the best way to allow organizations to team up and become more innovative in their ideas so that they can achieve the goals they have set.

TQM contributes to 83.1 percent of process and product innovation (Long et al. 2015). Thus, TQM will not pose an obstacle to innovation in providing new products, processes, and services, as new and improved methods can be used to achieve greater business effectiveness and efficiency.

Through its practices, leadership, continuous improvement, teamwork, and customer focus, TQM aims to improve the quality of enterprise management and enhance the organization's competitiveness and the value provided to customers. As a result, quality and innovation are not in conflict; instead, they are more intimate. When linking innovation processes to a quality system, we realize both are defending and supporting each other in a friendly relationship. Quality management is the systematic framework that promotes innovation values and establishes the basis for all operations throughout the organization. In fact, Zeng et al. (2015) indicated that quality and innovation can co-exist in a cumulative model using quality as the foundation.

The key elements that are common to both quality management and innovation include ongoing improvement, employee participation in decision-making, support from top management, teamwork, and having an open culture (Fernandes et al. 2014). This is in line with a study by Zhang et al. (2016) wherein the authors identified the key elements of a quality management infrastructure and quality management practices that have a profound impact on innovation as consisting of the commitment of top management, the involvement of employees, and a focus on customers, continuous improvement, efficiency in process flow management, and superior relationships.

2.3 Bringing in Tools: What Can We Learn from Total Quality Management (TQM) to Innovate?

Quality may be defined in various in-depth perspectives, but in simple terms, it is the way we reach out to people, understand them and their needs, and help them build their business by being a part of it indirectly via continuous improvement to minute details. Innovation can be understood as evolved quality thinking, even though it could contradict some quality practices (Asq.org 2018). However, organizations are mutually exclusive to organizations. Quality management emphasizes continuous improvement to satisfy existing customers, whereas innovation management focuses on breakthroughs in products, processes, or services with an emphasis on gaining new customers (Leavengood et al. 2012).

Studies investigating the connection between TQM and innovation performance are important because they provide a theoretically supported platform for organizations (Long et al. 2015). The lack of research into how quality management affects innovation has resulted in corresponding problems with innovation in organizations. Innovations in organizations are inhibited because of a lack of research into how quality management is linked to innovation (Chong and Randus). Quality can be perceived as multidimensional in nature and as including customer satisfaction, durability, and reliability (Long et al. 2015). Long et al. (2015) deemed at least three key principles (i.e. people management, customer focus, and process management) as being crucial to foster innovativeness in an organization. Additionally, Prajogo and Sohal (2003) and Long et al. (2015) showed that customer focus as a quality management practice is directly linked to organizational innovativeness. Studies have mostly found a strong relationship between quality management and innovativeness (Ardestani and Amirzadeh 2014; Bon and Mustafa 2013). Therefore, quality management can be viewed as interdependently linked to innovativeness as both approaches exhibit traits of mutual benefits. In other words, quality management can be used to foster innovation while innovation can also be used to improve quality management processes and practices. TQM is an administrative practice that provides a better performance for organizations (López-Mielgo et al. 2009). Although there are contradictory arguments regarding the relationship between numerous quality practices and innovation (Zeng et al. 2015), TQM includes a set of ideas and techniques aimed at continuously improving product and process attributes.

A study by Kim et al. (2012) investigated the relationship between quality management practices and innovation. Their findings revealed that a set of quality management practices has a positive relationship with five types of innovation: radical product, radical process, incremental product, incremental process, and administrative innovation. Organizational innovation and institutional innovation concern the creation of new adaptive methods to improve production, teamwork, and quality management. Marketing innovation relates to the application of new marketing methods that play a big role in changing aesthetic aspects of an organization, including packing, packaging, distribution, and marketing of products and services with modern technologies and the media. Concerning Research & Development (R &D) and technological innovation, all institutions should establish a department that cares about education and development to improve and develop existing services and products and to create a marketing environment according to customer expectations and in line with the labor market. Finally, management innovation addresses the development of modern management applications, the improvement of motivation, the introduction of modern technology, and the implementation of management strategies based on facts and knowledge. In fact, any organization in the world (e.g. Motorola and Xerox) should be utilizing quality management practices as a way of fostering innovativeness among its employees and in its production processes.

According to Kafetzopoulos et al. (2015), organizations that implement quality management practices and approaches tend to be more innovative in nature as they keep working toward the best product or service quality, encouraging their R&D team to provide innovative ways to maintain quality fit for the current market trends and demands. Although innovation allows companies to adapt quickly, finding new ways to handle market conditions and thus protect themselves from market uncertainty, they cannot be successful if their innovated products do not meet an acceptable quality standard.

Integrating and achieving a balance between improved quality and increased innovation is not an easy task. Most organizations focus on quality control; however, there is a high demand to be innovative. It is necessary to integrate innovation activities under the umbrella of TQM ideologies (Augusto et al. 2014).

Quality management is concerned with supervising all activities and tasks that an organization needs to maintain its chosen level of excellence. These activities may involve developing policy, creating and enforcing fine planning, and focusing on control and improvement. Innovation is a process that results in the growth of an idea into an excellent product or some sort of carrier for which customers pay.

Social quality management can result in improvements to product innovation. When an organization provides quality training, the result can be enhanced skills for employees and more efficient, effective teamwork among organizational members. Product innovation relies on creativity, communication, and cooperation. Information-sharing about innovative products grows from the types of exceptional relationships arising from quality management within the supply chain network. Augusto et al. (2014) explained that innovative products allow a company to reduce the amount of time spent developing commodities and increase their efforts on pursuing more innovation.

Interestingly, research has revealed that some parts of quality management (e.g. leadership) can facilitate the development of innovative ideas and products as well as improve problem-solving on the part of employees. Some scholars have identified a significant positive relationship between performance and innovation, and they have asserted that a focus on customers is an essential part of quality management. Quality management can target several kinds of changes, such as technological versus organizational innovation, product versus process innovation, and incremental versus dominant innovation.

Asif and de Vries (2015) stated that the philosophy of management known as quality management practices works with all of an organization's functions concerning performance improvement and any changes to improve product quality. Camisón and Puig-Denia (2016) stated that quality management and innovation are core factors of an organization's sustainability. However, quality management also affects innovation. With the help of quality management, an organizational environment can be created that leads to the generation of more innovative ideas.

Quality principles can promote innovation as described below.

- Management Leadership: The organization should have a strong leader who promotes quality and innovation.
- Employee Involvement: When implementing TQM practices, the organization should involve employees, which will encourage them to innovate.

- Employee Empowerment: The organization should empower employees to take part in TQM implementation because it will motivate them to take risks, resulting in innovation.
- Information and Analysis: The organization should work to gather the right information from customers, competitors, and suppliers. In fact, the prestigious quality award MBNQA has named this as a key criterion.
- Training and Education: The organization should train its employees, which will improve both TQM practice implementation and innovative idea generation.
- Customer Focus: The organization should focus on what customers need and want as this will result in an innovative.
- Continuous Improvement: The organization should strive for continuous improvement because it will support a focus on customers and the improvement of teamwork. Together, these three elements lead to innovation.

2.4 Power of Ability, Opportunity, and Motivation (AMO)

Innovations often fail in the marketplace despite their benefits to the economy and to firms (Mahajan et al. 2000). This is why it is important for innovation deployment to be assessed through an effective framework to reduce failure rates and to continuously improve an organization's innovations. This calls for a theory-based framework that can guide organizational performance. As the TQM approach links to innovations in organizations, innovation orientation can be further enhanced through an AMO framework, which draws on basic concepts of psychology. First, we will explain the AMO framework and its relevance to our framework. Under the AMO framework, ability encompasses skills and capabilities essential to the performance of a behavior, motivation is the incentive toward a behavior, and opportunity refers to contextual and situational constraints relevant to the performance of the behavior (Trost et al. 2016). Given that innovation is a complex, multilevel, and emergent phenomenon that requires skillful leadership to maximize the benefits of new and improved ways of working, the theoretical footing of the AMO framework provides a basis for the assessment framework we will introduce in Chap. 3. According to the AMO theory, opportunity, motivation, and ability are crucial elements of a performance and may be the building blocks of any successful action. Lawson and Potter (2012) contended that applying the AMO framework may help overcome an organization's internal stickiness in knowledge transfer. Ability and motivation underpin an opportunity, in the sense that these factors can lead to the execution of an opportunity.

Innovation mainly stem from employees' willingness to provide solutions that help an organization capture such opportunities. The AMO perspective provides great insight into how to mobilize opportunities (Prajogo and Sohal 2003; Schniederjans and Schniederjans 2015) and clarifies factors that capture opportunities for innovation that emerge from creative minds in the organization.

Organizations need to increase employees' abilities, motivation, and opportunities to participate if they are to effectively enhance employees' innovative behavior (Schimansky 2014). Ability refers to the talent, knowledge, skills, proficiency, and experience required to achieve a task. Motivation refers to the willingness (or the degree to which an individual is motivated) to perform it. Chang et al. (2012, p. 929) defined opportunity seeking as "the search and utilization of resources and opportunities through social relationships to solve difficulties in transferring knowledge." According to Nahapiet and Ghoshal (1998), the ability of organizations to generate new knowledge and apply its results stems from the collective ability of organizational members to generate, learn, understand, share, and utilize knowledge.

Tho and Trang (2015) maintained that motivation helps individuals establish and improve the quality of cognitive engagement, leading to success. Ability, motivation, and opportunity have been identified in relation to specific tasks. For example, motivation to learn refers to "a desire on the part of trainees to learn the content of the training program" (Colquitt and Simmering, 1998, p. 654). Motivation is considered an important force in steering behavior toward desirable outcomes (Boudreau et al. 2003). This concept includes factors such as willingness, readiness, interest, or desire (MacInnis et al. 1991), which set a person or organization up for action in terms of the effort they are willing to exercise if they can see the benefits.

The AMO perspective has been extensively used in existing studies (Blumberg and Pringle 1982; Boudreau et al. 2003; Turner and Pennington 2015). Particularly, it has been used to illustrate knowledge transfer, network, and ties. For example, Chang et al. employed opportunity seeking, motivation, and ability as three dimensions of knowledge transfer competence and found they jointly determine the effectiveness of knowledge transfer in the subsidiaries of multinational firms (Prajogo and Sohal 2003). Reinholt et al. (2011) used this perspective to investigate why a central network position is not enough to ensure knowledge sharing in networks (Schniederjans and Schniederjans 2015). They took motivation and ability to share knowledge as the moderators of the linkage of network position to knowledge sharing and reported that knowledge sharing is the highest when network centrality, autonomous motivation, and ability all are high. Similarly, other studies have noted that the AMO framework has been applied to a number of areas within the management arena to investigate consumer behavior and decision-making (MacInnis et al. 1991), risk analysis and information-sharing at the firm level (Wu et al. 2004), opportunity recognition (Bendoly and Hur 2007), and the activation and influence of social marketing (Binney et al. 2006).

Drawing on the AMO perspective, our 4C component framework has components that are used for innovation deployments: Leadership, people, dynamic capability-building, and innovation outcomes. Our 4C framework posits that a firm can leverage leadership to foster innovation. Leaders' support is crucial because, when levels of motivation are low, leaders must provide support in order to achieve high levels of innovation performance. Leaders can influence employees' motivation (efficacy beliefs) by communicating a high level of confidence in the team's ability to achieve ambitious collective goals, and their confidence can have a contagious effect on members' own confidence (Podsakoff et al. 1990). Leaders also influence employees' abilities by providing a supportive environment to promote change. Finally, leaders influence opportunities by showing concern for members' needs, which promotes a belief among team members that the leader will provide them with necessary support

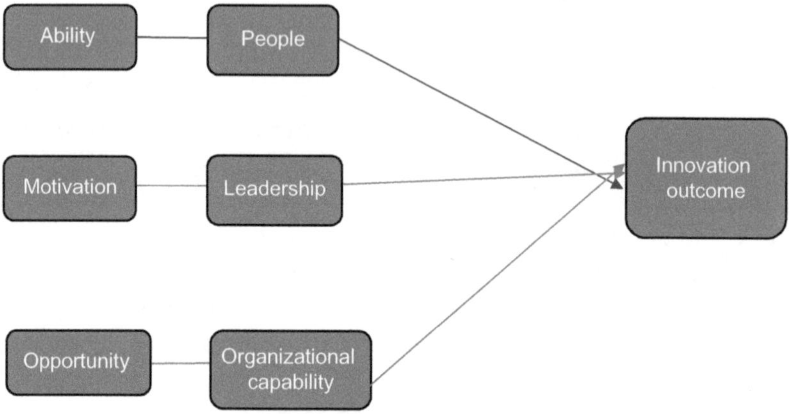

Fig. 2.1 The AMO framework and its linkages to the 4c model

and strengthens team members' confidence in their conjoint capabilities (Schaubroeck et al. 2007), thereby leading to improved outcomes.

A similar ability lies in developing the people who are the source of innovation. Additionally, Hutchinson (2013) argued that ability can be influenced by training, learning, and development as well as by recruitment and selection to ensure that capable employees are recruited in the first instance. Motivation can be influenced by extrinsic (e.g. financial) and intrinsic rewards (e.g. interesting work), performance reviews, feedback, and work–life balance. Opportunity can be influenced by communication, involvement initiatives, team working, and autonomy.

Opportunity concerns situations in which the benefits of acting toward a certain goal are clearly discernible. The individual or firm might be willing to work toward a goal, but they may not have the means to do so. Thus, it is necessary to understand how conducive a given context or situation is to realizing the identified opportunity as shown in Fig. 2.1.

2.5 Conclusion

Innovation, the profitable exploitation of ideas, has an important role to play in seeking competitive advantage. Innovation is a resource that can be realized in a firm, but it is intangible (Fernandes and Lourenço 2011).

In recent years, the basis for sustainable competitive advantage has shifted from high quality to innovation as society has become more knowledge-based. Bon et al. (2012) stated that "innovation is doing things differently while quality management is doing things in a better way." Numerous scholars have linked organizational innovation to technical quality management. These scholars have argued that the implementation of quality management practices including design for manufacturability helps in developing innovative plans internally alongside helping in the production of innovative products and services. Quality management and innovation are connected in many ways. Organizations that wish to change need both skills and knowledge, which are also critical for quality improvement and innovation. Consequently, studies have shown that quality enhancement results in innovation and vice versa.

Organizations can participate in fast product innovation only if they have completely considered every element of quality. Entering the market with poor quality will only harm the organization. In order to succeed in fast product innovation while keeping the highest quality in mind, the organization needs complete support internally.

Research exploring quality–innovation linkages has suggested that quality is essential but insufficient in today's business environment. An organization's long-term success depends on the firm's ability to innovate as well. As such, we do not embrace the perspective of which is more important: managing for quality or for innovation. Instead, we hold that quality and innovation go hand-in-hand and organizations can achieve benefits by driving them together. In fact, how quality relates to innovation and the propositions along this line have been tested. For example, quality management focuses on incremental improvement and satisfying existing customers—in other words, doing things better. Innovation is doing things differently, emphasizing breakthrough improvement and focusing on acquiring new customers. However, researchers have found strong linkages between product quality and process innovation.

Although disruptive innovations such as Google or Federal Express are all radical in nature and the focus of media attention, it is important to know that incremental innovation can also be lucrative and is necessary for long-term business success. Hence, quality and continuous improvement will always remain crucial to innovation (Hoerl and Gardner 2010).

References

Ardestani, A., and Y. Amirzadeh. 2014. The Impact of Total Quality Management Practices on Innovation Performance and Organizational Performance. *Indian Journal of Fundamental and Applied Life Sciences* 4: 2050–2057.

Asif, M., and H.J. de Vries. 2015. Creating Ambidexterity through Quality Management. *Total Quality Management & Business Excellence* 26 (11–12): 1226–1241.

Asq.org. (2018). Total Quality Management (TQM): What Is TQM? http://asq.org/learn-about-quality/total-quality-management/overview/overview.html. Accessed 4 Mar 2018.

Augusto, M., J. Lisboa, and M. Yasin. 2014. Organisational Performance and Innovation in the Context of a Total Quality Management Philosophy: An Empirical Investigation. *Total Quality Management & Business Excellence* 25 (9–10): 1141–1155.

Bendoly, E., and D. Hur. 2007. Bipolarity in Reactions to Operational 'Constraints': OM Bugs Under an OB Lens. *Journal of Operations Management* 25 (1): 1–13.

Binney, Wayne, John Hall, and Peter Oppenheim. 2006. The Nature and Influence of Motivation Within the MOA Framework: Implications for Social Marketing. *International Journal of Nonprofit and Voluntary Sector Marketing* 11 (4): 289–301.

Blumberg, M., and C.D. Pringle. 1982. The Missing Opportunity in Organizational Research: Some Implications for a Theory of Work Performance. *Academy of Management Review* 7: 560–569.

Bon, A.T., and E.M. Mustafa. 2013. Impact of Total Quality Management on Innovation in Service Organizations: Literature Review and New Conceptual Framework. *Procedia Engineering* 53: 516–529.

Boudreau, J., W. Hopp, J.O. McClain, and L.J. Thomas. 2003. On the Interface Between Operations and Human Resources Management. *Manufacturing & Service Operations Management* 5 (3): 179–202.

Camisón, C., and A. Puig-Denia. 2016. Are Quality Management Practices Enough to Improve Process Innovation? *International Journal of Production Research* 54 (10): 2875–2894.

Chang, Y.Y., Y. Gong, and M.W. Peng. 2012. Expatriate Knowledge Transfer, Subsidiary Absorptive Capacity, and Subsidiary Performance. *Academy of Management Journal* 55: 927–948.

Colquitt, J.A., and M.J. Simmering. 1998. Conscientiousness, Goal Orientation, and Motivation to Learn During the Learning Process: A Longitudinal Study. *Journal of Applied Psychology* 83: 654–665. https://doi.org/10.1037//0021-9010.83.4.654.

Doeleman, H.J., S. Ten Have, and C.T.B. Ahaus. 2014. Empirical Evidence on Applying the European Foundation for Quality Management Excellence Model: A Literature Review. *Total Quality Management & Business Excellence* 25 (5–6): 439–460.

Fernandes, A.A.C.M., and L. Lourenço. 2011. Quality, Innovation, and Performance: An Exploratory Study. European Concurrent Engineering Conference.

Fernandes, A.A.C.M., L.A.N. Lourenco, and M.J.A.M. Silva. 2014. Influence of Quality Management on the Innovative Performance. *Review of Business Management* 16 (53): 575–593.

Hoerl, R.W., and M.M. Gardner. 2010. Lean six sigma, creativity, and innovation. *International Journal of Lean Six Sigma* 1 (1): 30–38.

Kafetzopoulos, D., K. Gotzamani, and V. Gkana. 2015. Relationship Between Quality Management, Innovation and Competitiveness. Evidence from Greek Companies. *Journal of Manufacturing Technology Management* 26 (8): 1177–1200.

Kim, D., V. Kumar, and U. Kumar. 2012. Relationship Between Quality Management Practices and Innovation. *Journal of Operations Management* 30: 295–315.

Leavengood, S., T. Anderson, and T. Daim. 2012. Exploring Linkage of Quality Management to Innovation. *Total Quality Management & Business Excellence* 25 (9–10): 1126–1140.

Leavengood, S.A., T.R. Anderson, and T.U. Daim. 2014. Exploring Linkage of Quality Management to Innovation. *Engineering and Technology Management* 50: 1–31.

Long, C.S., M.H. Abdul Aziz, T.O. Kowang, and W.K.W. Ismail. 2015. Impact of TQM Practices on Innovation Performance Among Manufacturing Companies in Malaysia. *South African Journal of Industrial Engineering* 26 (1): 75–85.

López-Mielgo, N., J. Montes-Peón, and C. Vázquez-Ordás. 2009. Are Quality and Innovation Management Conflicting Activities? *Technovation* 29 (8): 537–545.

MacInnis, Deborah J., Christine Moorman, and Bernard J. Jaworski. 1991. Enhancing and Measuring Consumers' Motivation, Opportunity, and Ability to Process Brand Information from Ads. *The Journal of Marketing* 55: 32–53.

Mahajan, V., E. Miller, and Y. Wind. 2000. Introduction. In *New Product Diffusion Models*, ed. V. Mahajan, E. Miller, and Y. Wind, ix. New York: Springer.

Nahapiet, J., and S. Ghoshal. 1998. Social Capital, Intellectual Capital, and the Organizational Advantage. *Academy of Management Review* 23: 242–266.

O'Neill, P., A. Sohal, and C.W. Teng. 2016. Quality Management Approaches and Their Impact on Firm's Financial Performance: An Australian Study. *International Journal of Production Economics* 171: 381–393.

Podsakoff, Philip M., Scott B. MacKenzie, Robert H. Moorman, and Richard Fetter. 1990. Transformational Leader Behaviors and Their Effects on Followers' Trust in Leader, Satisfaction, and Organizational Citizenship Behaviors. *The Leadership Quarterly* 1 (2): 107–142.

Prajogo, D.I., and A.S. Sohal. 2003. The Relationship Between TQM Practices, Quality Performance, and Innovation Performance: An Empirical Examination. *International Journal of Quality & Reliability Management* 20 (8): 901–918.

Reinholt, M., T. Pedersen, and N.J. Foss. 2011. Why a Central Network Position Isn't Enough: The Role of Motivation and Ability for Knowledge Sharing in Employee Networks. *Academy of Management Journal* 54: 1277–1297.

Schaubroeck, John, Simon S.K. Lam, and Sandra E. Cha. 2007. Embracing Transformational Leadership: Team Values and the Impact of Leader Behavior on Team Performance. *Journal of Applied Psychology* 92 (4): 1020.

Schimansky, Schirin. 2014. The Effect of a High-Commitment Work System on Innovative Behavior of Employees. BA Thesis, University of Twente.

Schniederjans, D., and M. Schniederjans. 2015. Quality Management and Innovation: New Insights on a Structural Contingency Framework. *International Journal of Quality Innovation* 1 (1): 1–20.

Tho, Nguyen Dinh, and Nguyen Thi Mai Trang. 2015. Can Knowledge Be Transferred from Business Schools to Business Organizations through In-Service Training Students? SEM and fsQCA Findings. *Journal of Business Research* 68 (6): 1332–1340.

Trost, J.K., M. Skerlavaj, and J. Anzengruber. 2016. The Ability-Motivation-Opportunity Framework for Team Innovation: Efficacy Beliefs, Proactive Personalities, Supportive Supervision and Team Innovation. *Economic and Business Review for Central and South-Eastern Europe* 18 (1): 77.

Turner, Tobin, and W. Wesley Pennington. 2015. Organizational Networks and the Process of Corporate Entrepreneurship: How the Motivation, Opportunity, and Ability to Act Affect Firm Knowledge, Learning, and Innovation. *Small Business Economics* 45 (2): 447–463.

Wu, Wann-Yih, Chwan-Yi Chiag, Ya-Jung Wu, and Hui-Ju Tu. 2004. The Influencing Factors of Commitment and Business Integration on Supply Chain Management. *Industrial Management & Data Systems* 104 (4): 322–333.

Zehir, C., Ö. Ertosun, S. Zehir, and B. Müceldilli. 2012. Total Quality Management Practices' Effects on Quality Performance and Innovative Performance. *Procedia – Social and Behavioral Sciences* 41: 273–280.

Zeng, J., C. Anh Phan, and Y. Matsui. 2015. The Impact of Hard and Soft Quality Management on Quality and Innovation Performance: An Empirical Study. *International Journal of Production Economics* 162: 216–226.

Zhang, Q., X. Feng, and X. Xiang. 2016. The Impact of Quality Management Practices on Innovation in China: The Moderating Effects of Market Turbulence. *American Journal of Industrial and Business Management* 6: 291–304.

3

A Framework for Assessing Innovation

3.1 Introduction

Forward-thinking companies integrate many strategies to foster innovation within their business models, but many firms remain uncertain about which levers best facilitate its implementation. A great way to assist these firms, then, is to provide an empirically valid framework that assesses the impact of various levers that the most innovative firms use to tap innovation. This chapter introduces a framework to guide firms seeking to improve their innovation performance. After all, innovation is a process that involves fine-tuning multiple factors that are crucial for achieving superior results. Earlier chapters focused on explaining the typical stages involved in creating a culture of innovation and how knowledge generation should be diffused. We observed that a pool of quality ideas forms a strong innovation base and that a number of enabling factors must be deployed to generate such a huge pool of ideas that, eventually, help an organization to derive useful outcomes. The assessment framework mainly focuses on identifying how innovation levers or enablers are deployed to achieve effective innovation-related outcomes.

The framework comprises two main components, namely enablers and outcomes. The model construction used a three-phase multimethod

F. Lasrado, *Fostering Creativity and Innovation*,
https://doi.org/10.1007/978-3-319-99121-4_3

research approach to derive the framework that is discussed in this chapter. The first phase of the approach, which involved desk studies and a literature review, identified underlying factors believed to have some impact in systematically channeling creativity into innovative services and products in an organization. The second phase of the study consisted of a scientific investigation to understand the robustness and reliability of these factors to inspire creativity and innovation. This phase used a questionnaire survey and sought expert opinions to derive the importance level of each factor, which resulted in identifying the clear enablers and the resulting outcomes. This was then followed by a series of activities that flowed to a third phase of the research.

3.2 Understanding Enablers and Outcomes

An assessment framework generally encompasses the triggers or drivers that must be fostered for an effective outcome. An outcome is an output or a result that an organization greatly values in determining its success. Based on this framework, organizations can assess how well are they doing in terms of their innovation deployment. The relationships between enablers will differ in terms of their impact on the results. This is because each enabler is unique to each organization depending on its innovation strategy, goals, objectives, and resources mobilized for innovation deployment. The desirable outcomes of innovation deployment should have several impacts on new products or services or improvement in processes that enable the organization to generate a new stream of revenue and earn profit. Moreover, an organization should be able to elevate its position in terms of delivering its goods and services to its customers.

Traditionally, innovation was measured by analyzing the inputs in each production process. Particularly for technological firms, the main measurement of innovation was the number of patents that the firm generated. In some cases, how much the firm spent on R&D and the size of the R&D department were noted. Beyond these traditional measures of innovation performance, one study revealed that corporate organization culture played a drastic role in the growth of innovative thinking (Wyld and Maurin 2009). However, in recent times, innovation success has been measured not only in terms of indicators pointing to profits alone but also in an organization's achievement and the satisfaction of its partners in sustaining those high results. Likewise, achieving sustainable results requires an organization to manage stakeholders' and partners' expectations. The most innovative organizations consider customer experience as a key aspect of their business, and they drive their competitive advantage. Precisely, engaging customers in the design of the products or services that they are likely to consume is crucial for innovation. In general creating customer experiences that truly delight customers, and effectively tackling pain points of customers can enhance customer happiness. Immersion is a growing trend in business and describes the way organizations lead several initiatives to immerse themselves in understanding customer needs. Bessant and Tidd (2007) indicated that it is more advantageous to involve customers, especially lead users, in the innovation process of highly novel services.

Aside from customers, employees are important partners whose happiness should be attained through complete engagement and participation. The impact of the innovation must also have a large impact on the community; hence, social impacts are also important in the process of understanding to what extent the innovation drive has obtained a sustainable outcome, rather than a simple output. Indeed, we achieve better results with better means, approaches, or systems. The nexus of this assessment framework is conceptualized as shown in Fig. 3.1.

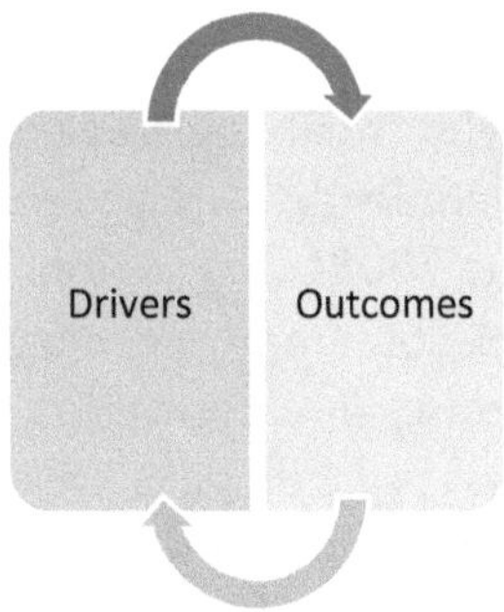

Fig. 3.1 Innovation framework

As Fig. 3.1 illustrates, drivers lead to the achievement of outcomes, and outcomes are strongly connected to the extent to which the drivers are optimized to achieve a superior performance. In the following sections, we will discuss the drivers or enablers that make up this assessment framework.

3.3 Component 1: Leadership

The most innovative companies teach us that leadership is a crucial element of innovation success in any organization. This is simply because the leader's support allows employees to be trained for success in the era of innovation. Leaders in innovative organizations use their leadership styles and thinking to inculcate a culture that shapes innovation. Innovative companies such as Apple, 3M, and ANP have exemplary leaders who have paved the way for innovation. Using longitudinal data from the US retail banking industry, Yadav et al. (2007) argued a positive relationship between the Chief Executive officers (CEOs)' attentional focus and innovation outcomes. They reported that the way in which CEOs carry out their discretion to assign scarce resources has significant implications for the firm's innovation outcomes over a long period.

This raises some debatable questions: How are leaders responsible for innovation? What roles does leadership play in a firm's emergence as an innovative organization? How do we understand whether leadership is capable of driving the trend of innovation for its organization?

In response to questions such as these, researchers have agreed that leaders are accountable for innovation in an organization. Studies have shown that leadership styles involving threats, intimidation, and coercive tactics appear to universally discourage creative behavior by employees (Anderson and Veillette 2008). A traditional, autocratic management style results in low levels of employee engagement and motivation (Hayward 2010). In contrast, an empowering leadership style can positively influence employees' psychological empowerment, an important element in affecting creative outcomes (Zhang and Bartol 2010). Therefore, the quality of leadership and their behavior toward subordinates has an impact on employee participation (Amabile et al. 2004; Egan 2005; Hayward 2010; Huang and Farh 2009; De Jong and Den Hartog 2007; Khairuzzaman et al. 2007; Marx 1995; Powell 2008; Zhang and Bartol 2010). Employees need support to try something new as they are naturally reluctant to make suggestions because they fear termination. Leaders, therefore, have a responsibility to satisfy this need for participation and create a culture that is supportive of employee involvement in the decisions that affect employees' work (Reychav and Sharkie 2010). As Binnewies et al. (2008) noted, such support can increase the quantity of ideas; conversely, in an environment with little support for creativity, older employees often stick to the routine way of solving problems and develop ideas that are less creative. Thus, the leadership–employee relationship can help the creativity practice to grow in the organization.

Leaders who want to drive innovation do not simply create followers but rather create the next level of leaders. Instituting leadership is crucial for innovative organizations because every individual in the organization has to make decisions to improvise in his or her own work. Only when these activities are exercised is creativity or innovation possible. Every employee should be embedded or trained in innovation-related programs, such as design thinking. Innovative companies have people trained in design thinking, which is a popular problem-solving method. Leaders are responsible for shaping the organization's culture toward design thinking, which empowers each employee to see the bigger picture and find alternative solutions. Leaders can institute trainings in design thinking or similar proven approaches to steer innovation progress.

In a case study-based research that we conducted to understand the leader's role, we were happy to root out a few dimensions that truly help to shape a leadership culture for innovation. The most prominent among these are: the extent to which leaders lend their support for innovation; their ability to manage co-creation or responsible for creating next-level (level 2) leaders; and the extent to which leaders create opportunities for innovation, plan and action support, and facilitate communication and networking. The following sections will examine these exemplary practices in greater detail.

3.3.1 Leaders' Support for Innovation

Leaders' support for innovation can take many forms. Because leaders are expected to be role models in the organization, their support for innovation can first be envisaged as being role models of innovation. In other words, employees observe the extent to which leaders encourage and participate in the innovation drive of the organization. Direct involvement and showing a keen interest in innovation are of utmost importance for leaders. On a personal level, leaders tend to be passionate about innovation and, in turn, become an example by walking the walk for innovation.

3.3.2 Relational Co-creation/Co-creation of Managers and Coworkers

Leaders are responsible for co-creation for innovation. Leaders facilitate co-creation by encouraging their subordinate level of management to work with their teams to foster innovation. Middle-level management is generally seen as taking fewer risks. Leaders must play a role in creating a scenario of co-creation or teams working together toward the goal of innovation. This is further achieved by bolstering coworkers' support of each other in taking risks and trying alternative solutions. Leaders must shape a work environment of co-creation or working together so that managers and employees co-create value for their organization, exhibit a high level of openness, and engage in open innovation.

It is vital that first-line managers work closely with their team, help them to develop ideas, guide their thinking, and assist them with getting ideas down on paper and testing them because many employees withhold good ideas when they discover their immediate supervisor feels threatened by their initiative. Moreover, an idea in isolation and with no close support from other functions will have very little chance of succeeding. Sustained performance is based on a resilient trust relationship associated with active involvement and support of both employees and management working together to make the program a success (Arthur and Kim 2005); hence, co-creation is important to nurture. Moreover, the useful feedback and support of coworkers enhances employee creativity (Madjar 2008;

Zhou and George 2001). McLean (2005) noted that an environment of freedom and autonomy is more likely to tap into employees' intrinsic motivation, which is a key factor in promoting creativity in organizations. Dissatisfied employees with high continuance commitment are more likely to be creative when their coworkers are helpful and supportive (Zhou and George 2001).

3.3.3 Create Opportunities for Innovation or Mobilizing Support

In highly innovate organizations, leaders have to take responsibility to support initiatives that foster creativity or innovation. They have to plan and provide support for creative ideas to reach their ends. When an idea emerges, nurturing and implementing it requires the leader's commitment to authorize and facilitate support systems and ensure due recognition of the employees for taking those necessary steps. Establishing management systems with ample interventions that induce and foster creativity are crucial responsibilities of innovation leaders.

As research has suggested, even in a field where innovation is essential, most acute challenges do not concern innovation skills, but rather the organizational context of innovation—that is, the work community's culture, habits, and practices (Björklund 2010). Organizational climate and cognitive-motivational-related factors such as motivation, trust, proactivity, and willingness to collaborate dominate the success factors (Björklund 2010). Creativity and innovation will be sporadic occurrences and will not thrive without a supportive environment and culture (Malaviya and Wadhwa 2005). In particular, an organizational structure that establishes rigid control often hinders tacit knowledge-sharing (Alwis and Hartmann 2008). Different industries may require modified organizational structures to support the transfer and transmission of tacit knowledge in the best way (Alwis and Hartmann 2008). Organizations should display an attitude toward employees "of putting people first," making managers at different levels accountable for using the system, establishing a clear employee orientation supported by a no-layoff policy (McConville 1990; Prather and Turrell 2002; Recht and Wilder 1998), and encouraging workers' self-initiative (Aoki 2008).

Moreover, the perceived work environment does make a difference in levels of creativity in organizations (Amabile et al. 1996). Some researchers have claimed that perceived organizational support is explicitly necessary for creativity stimulation (Zhou and George 2001). These are true action points for the leadership to keep a tab on. Companies aspiring toward innovative goals need to learn from the examples of highly successful companies like 3M and The Body Shop whose leaders spend their energy and effort in building organizational cultures and climates that perpetually create innovation (Ahmed 1998).

Empowering leadership has the capacity to positively influence employees' psychological empowerment (Zhang and Bartol 2010). Amabile et al. (2004) remarked that a leader who interacts daily with subordinates may, through certain behaviors directed at those subordinates, influence their daily perceptions, feelings, and performance, ultimately influencing the overall creativity of the work that they do. Leaders display support for subordinates and their work by monitoring progress efficiently and fairly, consulting with them on important decisions, supporting them emotionally, and recognizing them for good work. They can aim at some deliberate actions to stimulate idea generation and, by their more general, daily behavior (De Jong and Den Hartog 2007). Thus, the leadership–employee relationship can help grow the creativity practice in the organization. Various organizational members, particularly those at lower levels who are in touch with customers and face the competitive environment, have the most creative ideas and have innovative tactics to solve problems (Beer et al. 2005, p. 19). Therefore, leaders must support, empower, and develop them to engage in problem-solving. Only when leadership exhibits its support by providing the necessary guidance and atmosphere can it assist and encourage employees to adjust to new changes needed for innovation (Carmeli et al. 2010).

3.3.4 Communication and Networking

Creativity in an organization emerges from a process of sharing information (Bakker et al. 2006). Of course, people need social, informational, and economic support to be able to create something new (Majdar 2005).

Researchers have also contended that creative ideas are more often the product of social interaction and influence, than of periods of thinking in isolation (Yuan and Zhou 2008). So, leaders have a role to play in improving communication and promoting and enhancing the sense of common purpose. Conversely, information-sharing with non-work-related individuals, who in general are not expected to possess domain-relevant knowledge, may influence creativity by facilitating remote associations and providing cognitive stimulation as well (Madjar 2008). Ideas that are not shared are ideas that never become revenue drivers (Hering and Phillips 2006). Björklund and Magnusson (2009) identified a significant interrelationship between providers' connectivity in the network and the quality of the innovation ideas generated. The authors found that the more connected category performed better than the least connected category. A free flow of information—both along the vertical axis and between units that belong to the same hierarchical level—helps ensure that information-sharing organizations are ripe for innovation success (Aoki 2008; Clark 2009; Khairuzzaman et al. 2007; Recht and Wildero 1998; Shalley and Gilson 2004; Stranne 1964).

The innovation literature has revealed that, to promote the efficiency of product development and contribute to firms' competitiveness, the multidisciplinary cooperative environments of firms, science, and technology institutions should coexist and collaborate (Alves et al. 2007). In fact, the way in which individuals and organizations collect, disseminate, exchange, and use information influences idea generation (Koc and Ceylan 2006). An article published in the *Human Resource Management International Digest* (2010) reported that the better benefits are communicated, the more the staff appreciates their employer. Additionally, even when employees do not take up benefit offers, engagement with the organization is increased through benefit communication. Rightly, a network alone cannot be considered as an important source of information for innovation (Bigliardi and Dormi 2009). High-quality social exchange relationships (Kudisch 2006), social influences (Klijn and Tomic 2010), collaboration (Björklund 2010; Fairbank and Williams 2001), and diverse group exchanges (Shalley and Gilson 2004) must exist to stimulate employee creativity. The flow of communication and social exchanges and networks are, therefore, enablers for the suggestion system as the initial idea concepts need discussion, interaction, and incubation (Hering and Phillips 2006).

In recent years, co-development with customers has attracted considerable interest as a means to improve companies' product innovativeness and performance (Maria Stock et al. 2017). Senior leadership has a responsibility to facilitate and leverage co-development though appropriate innovation strategies. Clearly, leaders have opportunities to capitalize on and facilitate such meaningful exchanges among employees.

In short, organizational leaders serve as role models and ensure the creation of supportive elements which may include aligning middle management, ensuring a co-creation environment, and facilitating multidirectional communication within the organization. Innovation leadership shapes a context that promotes a capacity to learn, change, and adapt in high-velocity environments (Beer et al. 2005).

In conclusion, a firm's leadership must exhibit its most suitable leadership style, plan and mobilize effective support, and foster a culture that is conducive to innovation by ensuring the right level of communication, social exchanges, and timely development of its employees take place. The involvement of customers and employees in co-creation must be well planned. The framework, thus, suggests several key questions to be raised to understand the extent to which leadership is effective in innovation deployment. These include:

- Are our leaders engaged in a leadership style that is empowering and participative?
- Are our leaders ensuring the full participation of the organization's employees in innovation through a conducive organizational environment?
- Are our leaders instituting leadership at the next level?
- Are our leaders able to manage co-creation in the organization with both customers and employees at all levels?
- Are our leaders effectively planning the resources, auctioning their support, and facilitating employee development?

The next question on our innovation journey should respond to the call for innovation: How do we develop our employees' skills and operationalize innovation?

3.4 Component 2: People

Innovation is a complex process because it depends on the interaction of people within an organization. People are sources of creativity, and the most innovative organizations have leveraged innovation through their people. An organization's shared ability is needed for innovation. As a result, firm-level innovation capability depends significantly on accumulated knowledge embedded in human resources, and this knowledge results from learning processes. The main contribution to innovation lies within the firm's people capabilities such as talent, knowledge, team structure, tools, and processes. Not surprisingly, Suzy Welch, co-founder of the Jack Welch Management Institute and a noted business journalist, TV commentator, and public speaker, mentioned in a CNBC interview that "top employers want confident candidates full of ideas and energy" (CNBC 2018). The people or employees in the organization are human beings whose imagination is the root of the organization's innovation. Such ability must be multiplied to result in a collective imagination that brings about superior performance. Having said that, people learn in an organic fashion and not simply through mechanistic processes, which means creativity needs to carefully nurtured. The collective imagination of people can be elucidated by creating necessary interventions. An employee's desire for participation can become the essence of innovation. As such, an organized innovation process that motivates employees to participate is crucial for innovation success. An organization should ask: How do we trigger or pull the people lever for innovation success? How can our organization thrive through its people?

An organization involves people from multiple levels, beginning with employees and continuing to other relevant stakeholders. The challenge, however, has been to elicit ideas and put them to use. Simply put, innovative organizations truly value their people. They believe that their employees' talent, knowledge, skill, passion, and dedication lead to the organization's success. As a result, they believe in their people and value their knowledge across the spectrum, from employees and supervisors to area representatives. These organizations also recognize that their continued success depends on their employees being involved and engaged in the business. Indirectly, a successful reputation for innovation will attract creative, enthusiastic people who will then form the foundation for future innovation and development (Steele and Murray 2004). Clearly, innovation in organizations depends on many things, one of which is the individuals who find, invent, or propose useful innovations (Monge et al. 1992).

As Hoyrup (2010) noted, "Innovation is driven by employees' resources: ideas, creativity, competence and problem-solving abilities. These innovative activities are embedded in employees' daily work activities – often in working teams – on the basis of their experience and on-the-job learning." So, creativity fuels the innovation pipeline (McLean 2005). Creative engagement occurs in individuals, in interaction between individuals, and in group work (Watson 2007). Carrier (1998) reported that most researchers consider organizational creativity to be fostered through personal characteristics and motivations of creative individuals. Employees need to be motivated and encouraged for their involvement, which can be increased if employees develop a sense of belonging to the organization (Cruz et al. 2009). One of the biggest reasons employees do not pass their ideas up the line is that no one asks them. The level of employee participation in decision-making is a strong indicator of willingness to engage in behavior that supports the organization. Leveraging employees' wisdom through effective motivational interventions such as rewards and recognition can have a significant impact on the innovation journey of an organization. Effectively engaging employees in innovation is not easy, and it requires several important interventions to be created, as described below.

3.4.1 Desire to Participate

Employees should have the desire and motivation to participate and be positively engaged with an organization for innovation to flourish. So, how do organizations create interventions to foster these elements? First, they should understand that good ideas can come from anyone, at any level, anyplace, and anytime (Majdar 2005; McConville 1990). Therefore, every staff member should be encouraged to innovate. Moreover, expertise is a significant factor in creativity (Bigliardi and Dormio 2009; Björklund 2010; Griffiths-hemans and Grover 2006; Klijn and Tomic 2010; Madjar 2005, 2008;

Verworn 2009). For example, one study found that innovation was greater in banks headed by more educated managers who came from diverse functional backgrounds (Bantel and Jackson 1989). Employees that have the information, power, and skill needed to make decisions on a wide range of issues are more creative (Axtell et al. 2000; De Jong and Den Hartog 2010; Lipponen et al. 2008; McLean 2005; Powell 2008; Unsworth 2005). As Amabile et al. (2004) noted, an individual's perceived work environment makes a difference in the level of creativity in organizations. Perceived organizational support (POS) refers to employees' perception of the organization's commitment to them and reflects their beliefs about the extent to which the organization values their contributions and cares about their well-being (Eisenberger et al. 1986). A study by Rhoades and Eisenberger (2002) indicated an association between POS, favorable job conditions, and three major categories of beneficial treatment received by employees: fairness, supervisor support, and organizational rewards. If employees form positive attitudes, perceptions, and take personal initiative, it would support the creative process and idea generation (Binnewies et al. 2007).

3.4.2 Building Employee Motivation

The question then arises: What can be done to motivate employees to be innovative? As Zhou and George (2001) noted, POS for creativity can play a positive role in channeling job dissatisfaction into creativity. Today's workforce is very demanding, and employees not only expect to be involved in an organization's decision-making process, but they also want to utilize their full potential (Kesting and Ulhoi 2010). Malaviya and Wadhwa (2005) reported that the effectiveness of an employee's contribution toward new knowledge useful for the company is dependent on the employee's perception of the organization.

Individuals tend to exhibit high creativity when their jobs are complex, their supervisors engage in supportive, non-controlling behaviors, and their work is evaluated in a developmental, non-judgmental fashion (Shalley et al. 2004). Moreover, environments where employees are encouraged to develop new ideas and participate in decisions are most likely to facilitate the actual implementation of ideas. Job attributes such as happiness, challenging jobs, work complexity, employee well-being, autonomy, and coworker support have been widely noted to improve the employee's creative ability. Happiness predicts creativity (Rego 2009). Individuals are more creative when they are interested in the task, when they enjoy the process of working on the task, and when they feel motivated primarily by the interest, enjoyment, satisfaction, and challenge of the work itself (Yuan and Zhou 2008). These findings suggest that, as long as employees experience a higher quality of work-life, their creativity will also remain high.

3.4.3 Opportunities for Collective Imagination

Teamwork is another core practice of innovative organizations. Team ideas generally have a higher value. As Ahmed (1998) highlighted, the most innovative companies of the future will undoubtedly be those that have built enduring environments of human communities striving toward innovation through the creation of appropriate cultures and climate rather than those that simply focus energies upon product and technical innovation. Amabile et al. (1996) noted that all innovation begins with creative ideas and that successful implementation of new programs, new product introductions, or new services depends on a person or a team having a good idea and developing that idea beyond its initial state. The organization benefits from team-based schemes, teamwork, and partnerships to promote the scheme and evaluate ideas with the involvement of staff representatives wherever possible (Amabile et al. 1996). Finally, organizations should also focus on building expertise for the collective imagination. Studies have shown that firms invest in training their employees to increase organizational competitiveness and profitability and to boost employee morale and behaviors. Malaviya and Wadhwa (2005) stated that, without a supportive environment and culture, creativity and innovation will be sporadic occurrences and will not thrive. As previously mentioned, how individuals and organizations collect, disseminate, exchange, and use information influences idea generation (Koc and Ceylan 2006); hence, an organized process to guide such transfer of knowledge is key to innovation success. Specifically, choosing the ideas for implementation must have appropriate criteria; if not, the innovation will suffer (Rietzschel et al. 2010). Based on these findings, the people enabler hints at the need to develop a workforce management system that leverages its employees to think freely, designs highly interactive work systems, creates routines and tasks with ample flexibility, and, more importantly, focuses on fully developing employees' skills and abilities. The insights gained through research and literature indicate that employee engagement is crucial in the innovation process. In recent years, firms have found novel means to overcome this limitation, one being profit-sharing schemes.

The case study research further gave insights to grow employees for innovation by building up their motivation, increasing their expertise in imagination, and introducing interventions for collective imagination. Specifically, the organization should pose questions such as these to understand the capability of people for innovation:

- Are our employees motivated to participate in innovation?
- Are our employees positively engaged with the organization?
- Are we emphasizing employee job factors such as happiness and well-being?
- Are we creating opportunities for our employees to work in teams?
- What opportunities exist to generate ideas in teams?
- Are we providing training to employees for innovation?
- Are we rewarding employees to be engaged in idea generation and exploitation?
- Are we encouraging all levels of employees to be actively involved in our innovation drive?

3.5 Component 3: Capability-Building

Undoubtedly, organizations are engaging in innovation to confront the challenges of the world today. Innovative organizations invest and build their capabilities by aligning a number of interrelated organizational elements. As innovative organizations, they neither want to fail, nor do they want other elements of the organization to fail. A good way to avoid failure is to build robust organizational capabilities to meet innovation challenges and establish a deeply rooted innovation culture that will assist the organization in managing and combating twenty-first-century challenges. As a result, the third pillar of this assessment framework illustrates good practices of dynamic capability-building. Prior to embarking on investigating those practices, it is also essential to understand the concept of organizational capability for innovation.

Teece et al. (1997) defined dynamic capabilities as the capacity to renew competences so as to achieve congruence with the changing business environment. This being said, organizations must also focus not only on aligning internal structures within their capabilities but also seeking fit between their dynamic capabilities and the external environment (Wildne et al. 2013). Grant (1997) defined capability as the capacity of a set of individual resources to perform some task or activity. Firm innovation capability is a meta-capability, which has been defined as capabilities of the learning-to-learn type (Collis 1994). Chandler et al. (1998) explained capability as "the potential ability of an organization to position itself in an arena of modernism such as new product development, technology and other advancements that result in competitive advantages over its rivals."

The literature has indicated that building such an innovation capability is key to the success of the innovation. Capability in innovative organizations involves attributes such as the ability to build a work environment supportive of innovation that presents a true sense of collaboration of its processes, places, and practices (3P). Such a 3P program is not new for innovative companies; for example, an innovative company such as IBM builds its capability through a 3P program. So, dynamic capability-building is critical for fostering innovation.

Bessant and Tidd (2007) developed a model aimed at assessing innovation management capabilities. Their assessment model comprised five innovation capacity dimensions: strategy, organization, processes, linkages, and learning. While all these components carry a significant value to diffuse the innovation, an organization must nurture them as to invoke the organization's ability to sense, size, and shape opportunities to direct its resources in developing a new product or service. Further, research insights have outlined several other organizational capabilities to diffuse innovation. Mainly, researchers have acknowledged that innovation warrants a culture that fosters collaborative routines and co-evolutionary learning emerging from customer involvement across the service innovation cycle (Bitner and Brown 2008; Simutupang and Sridharan 2005). Among the other strategic resources needed for the organization are the customers because they contribute to company growth (Zander and Zander 2005), so organizations should use them to shape innovation. Most popularly, customers are engaged in the form of co-creation. Such co-creation is important because, as Prahalad (2004) explained, today's consumers are more informed and are more connected with the global world and they feel empowered. In fact, Millennials want to participate in the design of the product they want to use. The act of customers providing input into the service design and delivery process extends the notion of co-production to co-creation of services (Lusch et al. 2009; Sampson and Chase 2010). Research has also suggested that organizations utilizing both internal and external sourcing of knowledge show better innovation performance than organizations relying on one or the other (Cassiman and Veugelers 2006).

According to the Oslo Manual (2005), several factors may hamper innovation activities. The factors fall into one of five groups: cost factors, knowledge factors, market factors, institutional factors, and other reasons for not innovating. Cost factors are, for example, lack of funds within the enterprise, lack of finance from sources outside the company, and excessive perceived risks. Knowledge factors include insufficient innovation potential, lack of information on technology, lack of information on markets, difficulty in finding cooperation partners, and organizational rigidities within the enterprise. Market factors include uncertain demand for innovative goods or services and a potential market dominated by an established firm. Institutional factors are a lack of infrastructure, weakness of property rights, legislation, regulations, and others. Other reasons for not innovating include factors such as not perceiving a need to innovate due to earlier innovations or sensing a lack of demand for novelty. The most common factor (approximately 56 percent) hampering innovation activities for enterprises in the Czech republic (CR) from 2010 to 2012 (Czech Statistical Office 2014) was a lack of financing within the business (Krause 2016).

In our framework of assessment, we focus on number of organizational capabilities that are crucial for innovation and discuss how to diffuse them. The framework thus involves 4Ps: process, places, practices, and partnerships alongside resources, co-development customers, strategy, and rewards and recognition. In the upcoming sections, we will discuss them at length, beginning with the 4Ps for innovation.

3.5.1 Process

Innovative organizations establish a sound process for innovation. Specifically, the knowledge possessed by individual employees can lead to a firm's competitive advantage only if employees have an opportunity to share and utilize their individual knowledge in ways that benefit the organization (Arthur and Kim 2005). In this sense, innovative organizations establish strategies, policies, processes, and structures for innovation. Significant obstacles in the innovation cycle lie in the area of review, evaluation, and guidance. When this aspect of the idea generation and implementation cycle functions properly, it can be a great motivating force that will attract many excellent proposals (Neagoe and Klein 2009). Dijk and Ende (2002) observed that organizational support and committed resources are required at three stages: idea generation, idea landing, and idea follow-up. When these requirements are met, a transfer will take place from employee creativity to practicable ideas, giving the organization a large and constant supply of relevant project ideas. In fact, an empirical study involving 331 Australian innovation managers revealed that the overall effectiveness of the innovation process was "significantly correlated with the effectiveness of idea assessment, suggesting that idea assessment is a very important phase of the innovation process" (Schulze et al. 2012, p. 11).

Organizations can milk their creativity process by engaging in competitive creation. In this case, the organization seeks to innovate through input from stakeholders during the co-creation process and therefore can gain significant control over their creative process. Crowdsourcing is one such method through which organizations can seek ideas through a competition (Howe 2008). This way of soliciting ideas from many contributions has benefits as these can be obtained at a relatively low cost and from a wide range of contributors.

Another type of user innovation mechanism is to involve users through online innovation tools, which can prompt users and customers to share experiences, spawn ideas, test products, or design products (Gangi et al. 2010; Prandelli et al. 2006). However, empowering users with tools and technologies has significant effects on the firm's capabilities as firms have to adapt to a new way of dealing with users and user knowledge (Ogawa and Piller 2006; Prahalad and Ramaswamy 2004).

3.5.2 Places

Beyond examining its process, it is important for organizations to create opportunities for hands-on experience or for prototyping. Therefore, places of such collaborative engagement are necessary for effective innovation organizations. Rightly, networks alone cannot be considered as an important source of information for innovation (Bigliardi and Dormi 2009). There must exist high-quality social exchange relationships (Kudisch 2006), social influences (Klijn and Tomic 2010), collaboration (Björklund 2010; Fairbank and Williams 2001), and diverse group exchanges (Shalley and Gilson 2004) to stimulate employee creativity.

Communication flow, social exchanges, and networks are enablers for innovation as the initial concept requires discussion, interaction, and incubation (Hering and Phillips 2006). That leads organizations to develop places to innovate where people can come together to discuss and share their ideas. The creation of such places in organizations can spur collaborative imagination. These may be thinking labs, experimental places, or even places where one can connect with the outside world to understand how innovation is being pursued. For example, an organization might provide access for individuals to listen to a creative approach such as that of design thinking. Regardless of how it is done, collaborative engagement must happen to drive innovation and performance.

Exploring how innovative organizations create such places has revealed that these places must be useful for their people and should be technology-enabled, well equipped with resources, and perhaps even open for outside access. Such facilities can undoubtedly help people to innovate. Knowledge places such as collaborative labs and communities of practice are critical for innovation as they enable a learning process that transcends the capabilities of an isolated firm. Managing organizational knowledge is viewed as a key driving force behind innovation (Malebra 2005). Therefore, organizations need to develop systems and processes for managing the knowledge exchange between the human and non-human entities, integrating knowledge from past innovation projects with current knowledge (De luca and Tuahene-Gima 2007).

3.5.3 Practices

As mentioned earlier, highly successful companies like 3M and The Body Shop have leaders who expend both energy and effort to build organizational cultures and climates that perpetually create innovation. Truly innovative organizations leverage good practices of building a culture of free thinking and driving out fear. Every organization has its own culture and needs, and it should be molded around adaptation for innovation. There are a host of good practices that organizations should embrace. In most cases, supportive organizational strategies and structures play a role (Alves et al. 2007; Alwis and Hartmann 2008; Bigliardi and Dormio 2009; Khairuzzaman et al. 2007; Shalley and Gilson 2004), and these factors may require modification based on the industry to ensure the effective transmission of knowledge (Alwis and Hartmann 2008). Even so, disagreements and conflicts may be useful for innovation, but organizations should make use of such environments effectively to create curiosity.

Organizational encouragement has been cited as an important factor (Bell 1997; McLean 2005; Van Dijk and Van den Ende 2002). Moreover, individuals are more creative when they are interested in the task, enjoy the process of working on the task, and feel motivated primarily by the interest, enjoyment, satisfaction, and challenge of the work itself. Career (1998) reported that employees experienced personal pride when the company accepted their ideas. This activity also fostered individualism and competition between employees. To be innovative, a company needs a department that innovates (Alecusan and Dimitrescu 2016).

However, a Japanese innovation survey (Kanama and Nishikawa 2017) administered as part of an empirical study to examine the impact of external factors on innovation outcomes produced some surprising results. The findings suggested that large companies tended to adversely impact the development of new products and services and their technological superiority when they offered monetary compensation, while the opposite was true with small or medium organizations. This impact could also be due to other related factors because large companies had varied ability to satisfy their employees' needs, which might not include compensation. However, this study also indicated that performance evaluation boosted innovation performance.

3.5.4 Partnerships

Birkinshaw et al. (2007) proposed that innovation networks evolve through three steps of finding, forming, and performing. In other words, individuals must choose the right partner and learn how to work with them before experiencing adequate performance.

An interesting observation also came from an empirical study conducted on IBM by Dahlander et al. (2016). The authors noted that, in a large organization like IBM, internal resources can be critical to generating novel ideas. Using a nationwide survey, Nogueira Tomas et al. (2014) showed that external integration with suppliers and customers is positively related to innovation outcomes and that radical innovation is directly related to large companies. It is a fact that organizations do not possess all the valuable knowledge internally; as a result, engaging with external sources is quite necessary (Chesbrough 2006, 2011). Moreover, ideas do not come from expert groups only, but also emanate from "non-experts" in communities of practice (Lave and Wenger 1991). Organizations learn from collaborating with others and engaging collectively.

The case study research gave some critical illustrations that also underlie innovation pursuit. For example, these center around how organizations take responsibility to celebrate quick wins, thereby showcasing the role models within the organizations. How are organograms designed? Do organizations have innovation-related roles? Are these roles tied around a robust strategy? Does the organization provide adequate resources?

3.5.5 Resources

Resources support the idea realization process. If organizations lack the necessary resources, even the best ideas will not be fruitful. Yuan and Zhou (2008) explained that an effective idea process is one that results in both numerous and novel ideas. An organized process is mostly evident in an innovative organization that guides idea collection, selection, evaluation, and implementation. The process not only ensures the smooth flow of ideas but also encourages collective participation through necessary innovation-friendly structures, policies, and allocation of resources. Organizational members have a clear responsibility and understanding of their role and the support provided to foster collective imagination. Among all technologies, IT has been cited as the most important enabler of service innovations (Randhawa and Scerri). Some of the IT-asked innovations include e-commerce through online retailers as well as social networking such as Facebook. As highlighted by Hana (2013, p. 84), various innovation initiatives in firms can influence competitiveness grounded on skills and abilities that are difficult to imitate. This suggests that innovation is an important element that drives competitive advantage among organizations by improving how firms use their resources and promote operational efficiency.

3.5.6 Co-development with Customers

Aside from resource use, Logue and Schweitzer (2015) explained that deep engagement with customers is key in an innovation process. Such engagement should be done either through an open-ended inquiry about the customer's needs or by extending a particular service offering. This engagement helps to extract the customer's tacit knowledge and vice versa. The organization can then use this knowledge to design or refine experience points, where the customer directly encounters outputs from the service. By engaging deeply with its customers, an organization can cover phases of prototyping, testing, and ongoing re-framing of the problem scope. After all, as Edwards et al. (2015) noted, building a co-innovation firm is not simple and requires putting the customer at the center of the business model—as a supplier, a producer, a tester, a marketer, a participant, and a consumer.

3.5.7 Strategy

In terms of innovation in medium and small companies, a major opportunity lies in the better administration and capitalization of employees' ideas. Such an initiative imposes a strategy for innovation management and a reward system for employees to encourage innovative behavior (Carmeli et al. 2010). An innovative culture fosters creativity among employees through informal communication, a positive work environment, and collaborative working arrangements that promote knowledge-sharing and learning required to generate new ideas on an ongoing basis (Hipp and Grupp 2005).

3.5.8 Rewards and Recognition

It is important to recognize that employees have to be rewarded and recognized for innovation culture to thrive and for employees to constantly find ways to improve and come together to build something new. These are essential for innovation cultures. As Du Plessis et al. (2008) noted, employees expect to be recognized or rewarded for their efforts and achievements in the organization on the basis of psychological contact with the organization. Hence, it is important that the higher-level authority in the organization ensures that they do not neglect the recognition, reward, and implementation of useable ideas. Suh and Shin (2008) explained that keeping workers intrinsically motivated is the key for improving creativity and performance. Intrinsic motivation is a universally important and substantial factor. Those individuals who are intrinsically motivated, have an innovative cognitive style, and have sufficient experience to carry out their work are more creative than those that do not simultaneously have these characteristics (Muñoz-Doyague 2008).

Reward is a key element. For example, a study by Toubia (2006) investigated whether carefully designed ideation incentives could improve creative output. He found that incentives have the capability to improve idea generation but noted that fear of evaluation and a feeling of free riding can undermine creative ability. In a study to determine what motivates employees, Islam and Ismail (2008) found that incentives play an important role in motivating Malaysian employees, irrespective of factors such as gender, race, or age group. Based on these findings, managers are expected to include all staff in their organization's reward and recognition system. A study conducted to understand the role of a reward system on knowledge-sharing by Bartol and Srivastava (2002) confirmed these findings. As Sweins and Jussila (2010) noted, one way to give employees a piece of the action is to involve them in the financial success of the business by engaging them in a profit-sharing system.

Arthur et al. (2010) analyzed the gain-sharing program at a manufacturing unit by studying the ideas made by its employees over a period of four years. They noted that the volume of employee ideas over time was positively related to the amount of payout received from a gain-sharing plan. Further, they reported that employee participation in the scheme was influenced by factors including the size and timing of the gain-sharing bonus payout, employee perceptions of fairness regarding the bonus payout, and positive, work-related, and work group communication. Consistently, rewards have been recognized as one of the most important motivating factors that would positively influence the success of the idea management system. Incentives are important for employees to feel that submission of their useable ideas will be rewarded (Du Plessis et al. 2008). As such, employees should not only be recognized for their ideas, but they should also be financially rewarded and awarded with presentations in-house and externally. The rewards should also reflect the value of the ideas to the company (Klijn and Tomic 2010).

In short, the third component of the framework (i.e. capability-building) emphasizes an organization's aptitude to embrace an innovation culture. The right mix of process, places, balanced practices, and partnerships along with resources, support, and rewards makes a huge impact on how innovation takes shape within an organization.

The key questions emerging in understanding the level of development in terms of dynamic capability-building include the following:

- Do we have an innovation strategy for our organization?
- Is our organization's culture conducive to innovation?
- Do we have the right structures in place to boost innovation?
- Do we have an organogram responsible for innovation tasks?

- Do our organizational structures provide the opportunity to innovate?
- How effective are we in terms of our process for innovation?
- What methods and approaches are in place to organize the creativity process?
- Is our idea pool captured and evaluated effectively?
- How soon and effectively do we organize to prototype our solutions and bring them to the market?
- Are we creating ample opportunities such as places within the organization to spur innovation?
- Are the resources adequate for employees to interact and test their imagination or increase their thinking ability?
- Are our innovation places being sufficiently resourced?
- How do we organize the funding for our projects?
- Do we set exclusive budgets for innovation?
- How efficient we are in making financial resources available for a timely action?
- Are we focusing on extracting appropriate knowledge through our partnerships?
- Are we effectively engaged with our customers in co-development and co-creation?

3.6 Component 4: Innovation Outcomes

The fourth component of the model is the innovation outcome. To understand innovation outcomes, a short introduction of innovation types is warranted, although this is not the goal of this book. According to Kim et al. (2012), there are five types of innovations: incremental product, incremental process, radical product, radical process, and administrative. Product innovation refers to changes at the end of providing products or services, while process innovation is described as changes in the way that an organization produces products or services. For example, one study (Czech Statistical Office 2014) reported the most significant results of process innovation activities to be improvement of manufacturing flexibility (57 percent), reduction of labor costs (15 percent), decrease of negative impacts on the environment (13 percent), expansion of production capacity

(8 percent), reduction of material and energy consumption (3 percent), and improvement in the health and safety of workers (5 percent). We broadly consider product- or process-related radical or incremental innovations as well as administrative innovations in this framework.

Second, it is also important to define output or outcome. Choi and Choi (2014) defined innovation outputs as the culmination of innovation processes, resulting in an improved product or service. Conversely, they defined innovation outcomes as the improvements in measurements of flexibility, effectiveness of service delivery, service cost, service quality, and client satisfaction achieved from the implementation of the innovation. Empirical studies have indicated that innovation outputs generally refer to the number of innovation sales, patents, and product announcements (Kempt et al. 2003). In our framework, we include outputs and outcomes, both of which are the results or the impacts created by the innovation.

Organizations measure different aspects of innovation outputs or outcomes. For example, innovation measures have included expenditures for R&D activities and the number of patents produced (Artz et al. 2010; Barreto and Kypreos 2004; Cassiman 2006; Enkel et al. 2009; Hidalgo and Molero 2009) However, today, the pillars that measure the degree of innovation no longer refer strictly to R&D costs or the number of patents and inventions. We include institutional, human and research capital, infrastructure, market environment, business environment, knowledge, and technology outputs as well as creative outputs when we refer to the assessment of the degree of innovation of companies (Bugnar et al. 2016).

In the context of service innovation, other types of measures have been used. For example, Agarwal and Selen (2011a) developed a multidimensional framework to measure service innovation. They identified a need to measure relational capital that drives network collaboration as a key lead indicator of service innovation. External forces linked with institutional, regulatory, and market competition dimensions are also key aspects to be included in the measurement of service innovation (Lee et al. 2009). Moreover, organizations are encouraged to implement innovations regardless of each innovation's success because the frequency of innovation activities appears to be positively associated with innovation outcome (Choi and Choi 2014). A successful measurement framework must assess areas such as the innovation's context (e.g. strategy and culture), lifecycle, and outcomes, as well as enabling factors (e.g. innovation actors and knowledge management). Metrics should be established to measure each dimension according to its main indicators. Organizations often struggle because they focus on measuring the inputs and outputs of innovation, such as evaluating their spending, the time it takes them to reach market, and how many new products they create. In the meantime, they ignore the processes occurring in between the inputs and the outputs.

The framework that we discussed addresses three key enablers and one outcome category that encompasses an understanding of the outputs and the outcomes. Innovation success is largely associated with achieving results that make a difference in solving the problems of humankind. Truly, innovations result in business outputs such as profitability and a number of stakeholder benefits, largely depending on the organization's purposes. Organizations' purposes may drive their outcomes to be "substantial improvement in quality," momentous process improvement, exceptional customer experience, and unparalleled employee-related achievements.

Case study research largely suggested that innovation should first connect to an economic outcome. Hence, an organization's profitability has a direct link to innovation. Innovative organizations should also exhibit results in the employee component. After all, it is the collective imagination that results in organizational innovation. So the practices of the employee's superior are results in the employee category. These are manifested in employee engagement or employee happiness. Happy employees are curious and better at making social contacts; therefore, they will make an effort and be ready to explore new areas (idesign).

Improvement in quality and processes is another strong predictor of innovative performance. Every new way of working is an opportunity to advance toward creating a greater customer experience. In today's world, we are witnessing the most challenging human generation, the members of which not only expect but also demand to take part in the design of the product or process they are likely to use. How an organization captures and creates these experiences can guide the innovation of a firm to a higher level. In fact, users or customers are considered to be the largest sources of innovation in many economic sectors (Bengtsson and Ryzhkova 2015).

The fourth component of the framework, thus, illustrates the importance of achieving the innovation results in these four broad categories. Organizations can design relevant indicators to capture and measure the results in such categories.

3.7 Preliminary Framework and Maturity Stages

The innovation assessment framework, which is comprised of four components (4C)—three enabler categories and innovation outcomes—is thus named the 4C Framework of Innovation Assessment. The components are to be assessed in relation to elements associated with each of them as shown in Table 3.1.

3.7.1 Understanding Maturity Levels

Having explained the 4C Framework of Innovation Assessment, we now explore how an organization can achieve an elevated status for its innovations. Indeed, variations always exist in how each of the enablers is fostered in an organization. The practices associated with each enabler element cannot be achieved through a mechanistic process. Moreover, organizations grow organically, as do their innovation elevations. Thus, fostering each enabler will vary not only from each other, but each enabler will also have a certain base level. From its base levels, enablers can move to the next gradual level; hence, the maturity of an innovation system is not simply a binary status of "yes" or "no." Innovation largely is about building a culture, and how we influence this culture varies based on the interplay of several enabler indicators. Eventually, how an organization manages to influence these indicators achieves a superior level of engagement for innovation. These culture shifts should happen as movements from a low score to a higher score on a scale. There are a host of approaches associated with implementing each of the innovation elements. These practices or approaches thus can be improved or developed beyond their initial stages to more advanced stages. Thus, the maturity levels can be

Table 3.1 The 4C framework of innovation assessment

Enablers	Elements	Description
Leadership	Leadership commitment and support	This indicates the commitment and support of top management to the innovation. The involvement and active participation of top management in innovation activities have a positive impact on the employees of the organization
	Communication and networking	Facilitating effective communication and providing employees strong support for internal as well as external networking
	Relationship co-creation	Ensuring that the managers and employees work in harmony and more through shared work responsibilities
	Mobilizing resources	Providing active support for providing resources to facilitate the innovation
People	Desire to participate	This implies the extent to which employees and engaged and involved
	Collective imagination	This addresses employees' opportunity to work in groups
	Expertise and training	This implies the extent to which an organization provides trainings to stimulate the creativity of employees and their ability to innovate effectively
	Building motivation	This addresses perceived organizational support
Capability-building	Process Idea creation or sourcing Internal processes Evaluation and prototypes	Capability indicates the provisions that the organization can make to support the innovation. This mainly includes
	Places Innovation Labs Collaborative platforms Co-sharing places	This indicates the extent to which the organization supports its employees with places and resources needed for developing and prototyping their ideas
	Practices Organizational structures Accountability and responsibility Innovation culture	This factor stresses the supportive elements that exist within the organization to support innovation. The existence and fostering of such elements is necessary for innovations
	Partnerships	This factor involves leveraging partnerships

(continued)

Table 3.1 (continued)

Enablers	Elements	Description
	Rewards and recognition	This implies the recognition and rewards that the organization allocates for innovation. Setting up a fair amount of rewards increases employee involvement in the innovation process
	Customer co-development	This implies the extent to which customer engages with its customers
	Resources	Extent to which organization provides necessary resources to provide support for innovation
	Strategy	Implies establishment of an innovation strategy
Outcomes		
Innovation outcomes	Profitability	These results show the financial gains achieved by the organization
	Employee experience	These results are obtained in the area of employees demonstrating employee experience
	Product quality	These results demonstrate elevation in the quality of products or services
	Process improvements	These results demonstrate enhancements in the process
	Customer experience	These results are obtained in the area of employees demonstrating employee experience Opportunities are created for co-development with customers
	Innovation projects or portfolios and frequency	These results show the initiatives undertaken and successful projects. These are mainly new prototypes created

understood as being at the initial stage, the developmental stage, or the advanced stage.

The initial stage is conceptualized as a beginning stage where there is little to no practices related to the factor indicators. Some adverse practices may also be present, negating the impact of an indicator at this stage. The developmental stage could be conceptualized as exhibiting adequate evidence for each of the indicators. In contrast, exhibiting good

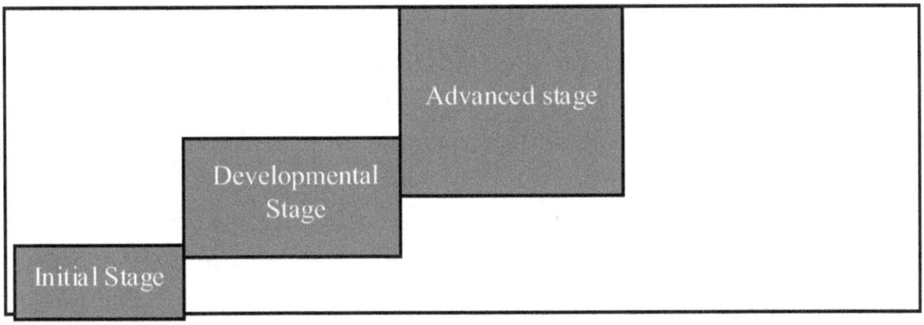

Fig. 3.2 Maturity stages

evidence in the form of a set of practices for each of the indicators implies an advanced status. Based on this understanding, we propose a three-stage model, as shown in Fig. 3.2.

Finally, it must be understood that maturity is to be built over time through an organic process. As a result, maturity is the ultimate goal, but starting the journey is crucial. It is not only warranted but needed for an organization's survival.

3.8 Conclusion

The chapter provided an overview of the 4C Framework of Innovation Assessment, which is comprised of three enablers (i.e. leadership, people, capability-building) and innovation outcomes as core elements of the assessment. Truly, as evidenced in this chapter, it is a challenge to lead a highly transformed organization of today into a drive for innovation. Organizations must nurture strong risk-taking behaviors for innovation success. In highly transformed organizations, leaders' challenge is no longer simply to create followers but to create next-level leaders. In a highly innovative organization, leaders have a responsibility to act as role models to accommodate a culture of risk-taking, to foster support, and to create a culture to leverage innovation by mobilizing necessary support and creating truly useful interventions under which innovation environments thrive. The leadership styles they adopt send out strong signals within the organization; hence, empowering leaders are generally able to leverage innovation cultures. They are also responsible for implementing communication channels and networking opportunities to facilitate and influence greater horizontal and vertical collaboration in the organization.

The second component of the framework is the people. An employee's desire for participation can become the essence of innovation. The shared abilities of an organization's people are needed for innovation. Better methods or approaches to encourage employees' abilities will produce better results. Fostering high levels of involvement and participation, empowerment, and competency as well as creating interventions for collaborative thinking, training, and building employees' expertise are key elements for leveraging the people enabler.

Third, capability-building is essential as innovative organizations want neither to fail nor to allow other elements of the organization to fail. A good way to avoid failure is to build the capabilities of the organization. There are several elements that should be leveraged to build an organization's capability, namely establishing a robust innovation process, creating places for open innovation, and developing highly enhanced practices that are necessary for innovation.

Fourth, results (i.e. outcomes) should be assessed in the pursuit of innovation. This framework aims to assess or evaluate outcomes including profitability, product quality, process advances, and employee and customer experiences.

Finally, we argue that leveraging each element is not a mechanistic process, so we conceptualize maturity as a three-stage model. The scaling of these practices matters, so the right mix of approaches and levels that an organization adopts may elevate its innovation from the initial stage to the developmental and eventually the advanced stage. Leveraging each enabler with robust and high-caliber influences can help achieve a superior level of innovation outcome.

Overall, the framework communicates one way of assessing innovation to support an organization in elevating its innovation status. There is indeed no one way to achieve results, and constant adoption and development with a shifting mind-set should eventually help an organization to achieve its desired results. Innovation is, of course, a great source of pride for an organization.

References

Ahmed, P.K. 1998. Culture and Climate for Innovation. *European Journal of Innovation Management* 1 (1): 30–43.

Alecusan, A.M., and A. Dimitrescu. 2016. Innovation Management: The Past, Present and Future of the Market. *Studies in Business and Economics* 11 (3): 140–149.

Alves, J., M.J. Marques, I. Saur, and P. Marques. 2007. Creativity and Innovation Through Multidisciplinary and Multisectoral Cooperation. *Creativity and Innovation Management* 16 (1): 27–34.

Alwis, R.S., and E. Hartmann. 2008. The Use of Tacit Knowledge Within Innovative Companies: Knowledge Management in Innovative Enterprises. *Journal of Knowledge Management* 12 (1): 133–147.

Amabile, T.M., R. Conti, H. Coon, J. Lazenby, and M. Herron. 1996. Assessing the Work Environment. *Academy of Management* 39 (5): 1154–1184.

Amabile, T.M., E.A. Schatzela, G.B. Monetaa, and S. Kramerb. 2004. Leader Behaviors and the Work Environment for Creativity: Perceived Leader Support. *Leadership Quarterly* 15 (1): 5–32.

Anderson, T.A., and A. Veillette. 2008. Contextual Inhibitors of Employee Creativity in Organizations: The Insulating Role of Creative Ability. *Group & Organization Management* 34 (3): 330–357.

Aoki, K. 2008. Transferring Japanese Activities to Overseas Plants in China. *International Journal of Operations & Production Management* 28 (6): 518–539.

Arthur, J.B., L. Aiman-smith, and J.E.F.B. Arthur. 2010. Gainsharing and Organizational Learning: Suggestions Over Time an Analysis of Employee. *Management* 44 (4): 737–754.

Axtell, C.M., D.J. Holman, K.L. Unsworth, T.D. WaU, and P.E. Waterson. 2000. Shop Floor Innovation: Facilitating the Suggestion and Implementation of Ideas. *Journal of Occupational and Organizational Psychology* 73 (3): 265–285.

Bantel, K.A., and S.E. Jackson. 1989. Top Management and Innovations in Banking: Does the Composition of the Top Team Make a Difference? *Strategic Management Journal* 10 (1): 107–124.

Bartol, K.M., and A. Srivastava. 2002. Encouraging Knowledge Sharing: The Role of Organizational Reward Systems. *Journal of Leadership & Organizational Studies* 9 (1): 64–76.

Beer, M., S.C. Voelpel, M. Leibold, and E.B. Tekie. 2005. Strategic Management as Organizational Learning: Developing Fit and Alignment Through a Disciplined Process. *Long Range Planning* 38: 445–465.

Bengtsson, L., and N. Ryzhkova. 2015. Managing Online User Co-creation in Service Innovation. In *The Handbook of Service Innovation*, ed. R. Agarwal, W. Selen, G. Roos, and R. Green. London: Springer.
Bessant, John, and Joe Tidd. 2007. *Innovation and Entrepreneurship*. John Wiley & Sons.
Bigliardi, B., and A.I. Dormio. 2009. An Empirical Investigation of Innovation Determinants in Food Machinery Enterprises. *European Journal of Innovation Management* 12 (2): 223–242.
Binnewies, C., S. Ohly, and C. Niessen. 2008. The Interplay Between Job Resources, Age and Idea Creativity. *Journal of Managerial Psychology* 23 (3): 437–457.
Binnewies, C., S. Ohly, and S. Sonnentag. 2007. Taking Personal Initiative and Communicating About Ideas: What is Important for the Creative Process and for Idea Creativity? *European Journal of Work and Organizational Psychology* 16 (4): 432–455.
Bugnar, N., L. Mester, and A. Fora. 2016. Innovation and International Competitiveness of a Country. *Annals of the University of Oradea, Economics Science Series* 25 (2): 35–43.
Carrier, C. 1998. Employee Creativity and Suggestion Systems Programs: An Empirical Study. *Creativity and Innovation Management* 7 (2): 62–72.
Carmeli, A., R. Gelbard, and D. Gefen. 2010. The Importance of Innovation Leadership in Cultivating Strategic Fit and Enhancing Firm Performance. *The Leadership Quarterly* 21 (3): 339–349.
Cassiman, B., and R. Veugelers. 2006. In Search of Complementarity in the Innovation Strategy: Internal R&D and External Knowledge Acquisition. *Management Science* 52: 68–82.
Chesbrough, H.W. 2011. *Open Services Innovation: Rethinking Your Business to Grow and Compete in a New Era*. San Francisco: Jossey-Bass.
Choi, S., and J.S. Choi. 2014. Dynamics of Innovation in Nonprofit Organizations: The Pathways from Innovativeness to Innovation Outcome. *Human Service Organizations: Management, Leadership & Governance* 38 (4): 360–373.
Clark, R.M. 2009. Are We Having Fun Yet? Creating a Motivating Work Environment. *Industrial and Commercial Training* 41 (1): 43–46.
CNBC. 2018. https://www.cnbc.com/2018/03/26/how-to-get-hired-at-amazon-google-and-other-top-companies.html
Czech Statistical Office. 2014. *Innovation Activities of Enterprises in the Czech Republic During Year 2010–2012*. Prague: Czech Statistical Office.
Dahlander, L., S. O'Mahony, and D.M. Gann. 2016. One Foot In, One Foot Out: How Does Individuals' External Search Breadth Affect Innovation Outcomes? *Strategic Management Journal* 37 (2): 280–302.

De Jong, J.P.J., and D.N. Den Hartog. 2007. How Leaders Influence Employees' Innovative Behavior. *European Journal of Innovation Management* 10 (1): 41–64.

De Jong, J., and D. Den Hartog. 2010. Measuring Innovative Work Behaviour. *Creativity and Innovation Management* 19 (1): 23–36.

Du Plessis, A.J., A.E. Marx, and G. Wilson. 2008. Generating Ideas and Managing Suggestion Systems in Organisations: Some Empirical Evidence. *International Journal of Knowledge, Culture and Change Management* 8 (4): 133–140.

Edwards, M., D. Logue, and J. Schweitzer. 2015. Towards an Understanding of Open Innovation in Services: Beyond the Firm and Towards Relational Co-creation. In *The Handbook of Service Innovation*, ed. R. Agarwal, W. Selen, G. Roos, and R. Green, 75–90. London: Springer.

Egan, T.M. 2005. Factors Influencing Individual Creativity in the Workplace: An Examination of Quantitative Empirical Research. *Advances in Developing Human Resources* 7 (2): 160–181.

Hayward, S. 2010. Engaging Employees Through Whole Leadership. *Strategic HR Review* 9 (3): 11–17.

Hipp, C., and H. Grupp. 2005. Innovation in the Service Sector: The Demand for Service-Specific Innovation Measurement Concepts and Typologies. *Research Policy* 34: 517–535.

Huang, J., and J. Farh. 2009. Employee Learning Orientation, Transformational Leadership, and Employee Creativity: The Mediating Role of Employee Creative Self-Efficacy. *Academy of Management Journal* 52 (4): 765–778.

Kanama, D., and K. Nishikawa. 2017. Does an Extrinsic Reward for R&D Employees Enhance Innovation Outcomes? Evidence from a Japanese Innovation Survey. *R&D Management* 47 (2): 198–211.

Kempt, R.G.M., M. Folkeringa, J.P.J. De Jong, and E.F.M. Wubben. 2003. Innovation and Firm Performance (Research Report H200207). Netherlands: Panteia/EIM Business and Policy Research.

Khairuzzaman, W., W. Ismail, and R. Abdmajid. 2007. Framework of the Culture of Innovation: A Revisit. *Jurnal Kemanusiaan* 9: 38–49.

Krause, J. 2016. Factors Hampering Innovation Activities: Case Study from the Czech Republic. *Journal of Technology Management & Innovation* 11 (4): 75–79.

Madjar, N. 2008. Emotional and Informational Support from Different Sources and Employee Creativity. *Journal of Occupational and Organizational Psychology* 81 (1): 83–100.

Malaviya, P., and S. Wadhwa. 2005. Innovation Management in Organizational Context: An Empirical Study. *Global Journal of Flexible Systems Management* 6 (2): 1–14.

Maria Stock, R., N.A. Zacharias, and A. Schnellbaecher. 2017. How Do Strategy and Leadership Styles Jointly Affect Co-development and Its Innovation Outcomes? *Journal of Product Innovation Management* 34 (2): 201–222.

Marx, A.E. 1995. Management Commitment for Successful Suggestion Systems. *Work Study* 44 (3): 16–18.

McLean, L.D. 2005. Organizational Culture's Influence on Creativity and Innovation: A Review of the Literature and Implications for Human Resource Development. *Advances in Developing Human Resources* 7 (2): 226–246.

Neagoe, L.N., and V.M. Klein. 2009. Employee Suggestion System (Kaizen Teian) the Bottom-Up Approach for Productivity Improvement. *Control* 10 (3): 26–27.

Nogueira Tomas, R., F. Pini Rosales, M. Otávio Batalha, and R. Lúcia Chicarelli Alcantara. 2014. Analyzing Effects of External Integration on Innovations Outcomes in Large and Non-large Brazilian Food Companies. *British Food Journal* 116 (6): 984–999.

Powell, S. 2008. The Management and Consumption of Organisational Creativity. *Journal of Consumer Marketing* 25 (3): 158–166.

Prahalad, C.K. 2004. The Co-Creation of Value—Invited Commentary. *Journal of Marketing* 68 (1): 23.

Reychav, I., and R. Sharkie. 2010. Trust: An Antecedent to Employee Extra-Role Behavior. *Journal of Intellectual Capital* 11 (2): 227–247.

Rietzschel, E.F., B.A. Nijstad, and W. Stroebe. 2010. The Selection of Creative Ideas After Individual Idea Generation: Choosing Between Creativity and Impact. *British Journal of Psychology* 101 (1): 47–68.

Schulze, T., M. Indulska, D. Geiger, and A. Korthaus. 2012. Idea Assessment in Open Innovation: A State of Practice. In *Proceedings of the 20th European Conference on Information Systems (ECIS)*, Barcelona, Paper 149.

Shalley, C.E., and L.L. Gilson. 2004. What Leaders Need to Know: A Review of Social and Contextual Factors That Can Foster or Hinder Creativity. *The Leadership Quarterly* 5 (1): 33–53.

Shalley, C.E., J. Zhou, and G.R. Oldham. 2004. The Effects of Personal and Contextual Characteristics on Creativity: Where Should We Go from Here? *Journal of Management* 30 (6): 933–958.

Toubia, O. 2006. Idea Generation, Creativity, and Incentives. *Marketing Science* 25 (5): 411–425.

Van Dijk, C., and J. Van den Ende. 2002. Suggestion System: Transferring Employee Creativity into Practicable Ideas. *R&D Management* 32 (5): 387–395.

Verworn, B. 2009. Does Age Have an Impact on Having Ideas? An Analysis of the Quantity and Quality of Ideas Submitted to a Suggestion System. *Creativity and Innovation Management* 18 (4): 326–334.

Wyld, David C., and Robert Maurin. 2009. Keys to Innovation: The Right Measures and The Right Culture? *The Academy of Management Perspectives* 23 (2): 96–98.

Yadav, M.S., J.C. Prabhu, and R.K. Chandy. 2007. Managing the Future: CEO Attention and Innovation Outcomes. *Journal of Marketing* 71 (4): 84–101.

Zhang, X., and K.M. Bartol. 2010. Linking Empowering Leadership and Employee Creativity: The Influence of Psychological Empowerment, Intrinsic Motivation, and Creative Process Engagement. *Academy of Management Journal* 53 (1): 107–128.

Zhou, J., and J. George. 2001. When Job Dissatisfaction Leads to Creativity: Encouraging the Expression of Voice. *Academy of Management Journal* 44 (4): 682–696.

4

"How Are We Doing?" Using a Maturity Model Assessment

4.1 Introduction

An old saying goes, "No measurement, no management." Our next question on the block is: How do we measure innovation performance? Innovation deployments should be measured and managed using a systematic process to sustain innovation and organizational growth. Moreover, innovation must occur consistently (El Bassiti and Ajhoun 2016). Despite its importance, measurement can weaken the spirit of creativity or the innovation process if the wrong things are measured at the wrong time using the wrong mechanism (El Bassiti and Ajhoun 2016). Existing research has also observed that assessment for innovation measurement provides somewhat useful metrics. Research of Adams et al. (2006) reported that the innovation management process consists of seven categories: inputs management, knowledge management, innovation strategy, organizational culture and structure, portfolio management, project management, and commercialization. Rightly, innovation measurements must not take into consideration a limited view of an organization's innovativeness but should measure its overall innovation capability (Muller et al. 2005). Interestingly, Kerka et al. (2009) observed

F. Lasrado, *Fostering Creativity and Innovation*,
https://doi.org/10.1007/978-3-319-99121-4_4

that about 6 percent of all gathered ideas and 14 percent of promising ideas that have reached the implementation stage have become commercial successes. However, when there are no past results for performance comparison or to prioritize the action plan for sustained results, the application of a framework helps as a starting point. The ready assessment tool described in this chapter will help organizations to conduct a systematic assessment of innovation deployment. Our assessment tool falls into the category of maturity models that describe the usual achievements possible at various stages of development along with multiple dimensions of innovation management. A number of maturity models describe achievement levels in relation to various deployment projects. For example, one well-known model was the Capability and Maturity Model Integration (CMMI) created by the Software Engineering Institute at Carnegie Mellon University. Similarly, we propose a maturity model of innovation deployment with three stages.

The purpose of this three-stage innovation maturity model is to allow organizations to evaluate how far they have progressed on their innovation deployment and to chart a path forward. Clearly, there are limitations when we consider undertaking an assessment simply based on a typical set of innovation questions or surveys. These do not necessarily help an organization to ascertain the facts beyond presenting some ideas that may not occur to them. Specifically, if there are no past results, the only way to measure success is to compare current results against the business objectives. In this chapter, we will review key aspects of our innovation maturity model, including its structure, application, and evaluation of its results. Our goal is to help an organization answer the following five questions:

- Does the organization have the right pieces in place to innovate?
- Is anything missing in the organization's innovation deployment?
- How well is the organization doing in terms of its deployment of innovation levers?
- What are the organization's challenges in innovation deployment?
- What is most important for the organization to consider in order to move to the next level of maturity?

4.2 Maturity Model Assessment Structure

In the last chapter, we described the 4C Framework of Innovation Assessment to evaluate innovation deployment. The four components of the model are leadership, people, capability-building, and innovation outcomes. In this chapter, we will discuss how an organization can use this assessment tool to conduct an evaluation and determine its maturity levels. The term *maturity* denotes the extent of an ability in performing a task or delivering an outcome (El Bassiti and Ajhoun 2016). Maturity in this context is defined as the level of innovation performance, which is determined by an organization's achievement of process- or product-related outcomes leading to organizational profitability, improved product or service quality, process enhancement, or added value to its stakeholder experience. The underlying practices associated with innovation levers and results will have to be analyzed to determine the maturity. The maturity model structure of CIAM innovation assessment has three stages: initial, developmental, and advanced, as shown in Table 4.1.

Overall, the assessment is positioned to ensure that:

- Innovation adds value to the organization by enhancing its products, services, or processes.
- Innovation increases the organization's profitability through its new offerings.
- The organization's environment is conducive to innovation.
- The organization has established the following dynamic capabilities to induce and sustain innovation outcomes:
  - timely risk-taking;
  - developing the next level of leaders;
  - strategy and process; and
  - resources, places, and practices.
- Innovations are frequent and continuous and are not occasional events.
- Co-development with customers and partnerships are strategic resources.
- Innovation has a social impact.

Table 4.1 Scoresheet for leadership enabler

Enabler indicators	Associated practices	Score
Leadership	Leaders act as role models	3
	Leaders institute leadership throughout the organization	3
	Leaders provide strategic directions and measure innovation performance	2
	Leaders consistently allocate the resources needed to fund staff innovation efforts	3
	Leaders support, empower, and develop their employees to engage them in problem-solving	3
Communication and networking	Leaders focus communication aspects of the organization to create maximum opportunities for employees to collaborate freely along horizontal and vertical axes and increase the opportunity for team-ups	3
	Leaders encourage team culture	1
	Leaders create communication opportunities and facilitate internal and external networking, driving toward high-quality exchanges between various elements of the organization	3
Relational creation/ co-creation	Leaders are engaged in building a relationship of co-creation among employees	4
	Few boundaries exist in leveraging their people to network, build internal or external partnerships, take initiative, and engage in decision-making processes at large	3
	Leaders ensure co-development with customers	2
Mobilize support	Leaders may have created partnerships and networks to leverage their innovation potential	2
	Leaders set up institutional budgets dedicated to taking on innovation projects	2
	Leaders use several collaborative opportunities such as crowdsourcing crowdfunding, and other initiatives to support innovation	4
	Leaders support and create events to increase creativity or facilitate relevant trainings	2
Total score		40

The assessment thus is structured around the four components based on the above broad aspects. However, it is unreasonable to expect that each organization should perform consistently across all the components. In fact, practices across the organization vary from one component to the next. The key is to assess the organization's strengths and weaknesses with regard to each component and build on its maturity. The three stages are described below.

4.2.1 Initial Stage

At an initial stage of innovation deployment, the practices associated with the 4C Framework of Innovation Assessment are unstructured and ill defined. Performance is unpredictable, and targets, if defined, are often missed. Budgets may not have been established, and funds associated with innovation drive may be haphazardly used. It may also be evident that basic processes are defined but are unclear, elementary, and very simple.

4.2.2 Developmental Stage

At this stage, the practices associated with the 4C Framework of Innovation Assessment allow for the organization to take responsibility for innovation. A creative and collaborative culture is somewhat in place. The organization has invested in building the basic infrastructure for innovation. There is evidence of some innovations taking place within the organization.

4.2.3 Advanced Stage

This stage represents the culmination of a successful innovation journey. Trust, mutual dependency, co-creation, co-development, and a creative and collaborative culture are firmly in place. There is a continued flow of innovations taking place in the organization, which has also gained a reputation for its innovation.

Table 4.2 shows the components of the 4C Framework of Innovation Assessment. Each component has subcomponents, for a total of twenty-five items. They make up the most important elements of innovation deployment. If an organization scores beyond one hundred points, it is

Table 4.2 Maturity table for leadership component

Score	Maturity level
<12	Initial
Between 12 and 30	Developmental
Above 30	Advanced

well it is performing well on its innovation journey. Unlike most maturity models, which generally have five levels of achievement or maturity from the initial stages with minimum efforts to world class, the 4C Framework of Innovation Assessment depicts only three stages. This is because ad hoc deployment and initial efforts are always necessary within an organization, and they indeed result in continuous improvement projects such as Six Sigma or gradual improvements. The goal here is to be prepared for some level of breakthrough innovations beyond improvement projects.

4.3 Creativity and Innovation Assessment Maturity (CIAM) Tool

In this section, we will discuss each enabler in relation to three stages of maturity. Maturity status is then determined based on a scoring of enablers and results. We will discuss each innovation-enabling factor in relation to the three stages.

4.3.1 Component 1: Leadership

What are the biggest challenges of today's leadership in significantly transformed organizations that have embraced great change and innovation? Truly, it is a daunting and challenging task to understand how leaders make a significant contribution to innovation deployment. One way to understand this is by examining how the leader's role has evolved in embracing innovation. As we discussed in Chap. 3, leadership support is crucial for innovation as the attention that leaders provide is directly related to innovation outcome. As a result, if the leadership lever is not fostered well, the organization can make the wrong decisions regarding all the other dimensions, namely people and capability-building, ending up with poor innovation outcomes.

Specifically, the assessment of leadership should focus on ascertaining the organization's commitment to, and support of, innovation. This may include establishing an innovation vision as well as goals, objectives, and strategies to achieve them. Simultaneously, leaders are responsible for allocating resources, creating communication, and facilitating networking of the organization's people internally and externally, driving toward high-quality exchanges between various organizational elements. For example, when the organization decides to thrive through innovation, then leadership has a responsibility to tie up partnerships to generate the resources that are needed to achieve the planned business results in line with the usage of time and energy necessary for the innovation. Similarly, leaders will have to focus the organization's communication aspects to create maximum opportunity for its employees to collaborate freely along both the horizontal and the vertical axes and increase the opportunity for team-ups. More importantly, if the organization's goal is to capitalize on innovations, leaders must be committed to being role models, as demonstrated by the most innovative companies, which have focused their energy in this direction. They may use a variety of styles to stir innovation suitable to their organizational culture, but their support should be manifested in their actions.

Beyond this responsibility, leadership must be engaged in building a relationship of co-creation. In other words, leaders should foster a value of co-creation by creating mutual agreements between managers and employees. They must understand the value of co-creation because innovation is mostly the result of such co-creation. Manager–employee and employer–employee partnerships should be established for individuals to work together and bring newness. Indeed, two heads are better than one; hence, collaboration and team structures should be well facilitated. Leaders' focus will largely be upon building more innovative subordinates rather than encouraging subordinates to simply execute assigned actions. True innovation leaders want to train their subordinates to think and take charge of their actions. Innovations thrive in such environments.

However, it is not possible for leaders to develop all of these qualities at once, and the development, in fact, goes through a very organic process. Good practices are developed as the organization matures. Typically, at the initial stage, leadership's role can be described as evidencing lighter commitment and support for innovation, showcasing basic levels of communication structures, and offering limited opportunities for employees to gather, network, and obtain necessary resources. In organizations at this stage, there may not be a sufficient push for employees to come together, and line authority may be strongly inherent. A silo system may still exist, only a small number of people may be engaged in innovation, or the deployment may be concentrated in only a portion of the organization.

At the developmental stage, leaders' support and commitment are well demonstrated through their actions, and leaders keenly participate in spreading innovation awareness and leveraging necessary resources. However, pitfalls may remain due to a lack of systemic processes or structures that guide the innovation. At this stage, the leader must make substantial investments to create cultures that are conducive to innovation and transformation to have a significant impact on the organization's outcomes. As such, the organization would have to devise a mechanism that would guide their deployment and refinements in relation to the results that they achieve. Leaders should focus on several developments that will elevate the innovation drive of the organization. Relational co-creation is visible during the developmental stage, and leaders have succeeded in removing some boundaries to leveraging their people to network, build internal or external partnerships, take initiative, and engage in decision-making processes at large.

At the advanced level, when organizations are mature, leaders are role models for innovation. They engage in innovation, and their focus is to institute leadership throughout the organization. In such environments, innovation thrives with no boundaries to collaboration and co-creation. Individuals have ample opportunity to gather ideas and gain support from the organizational system. Matured processes will be a guide, and leaders will take responsibility to regularly act upon the interventions needed to spur innovation. Leaders may have created partnerships and networks to leverage their innovation potential by creating opportunities to partner and work together to drive innovation. Typically, organizations may use several collaborative opportunities such as crowdsourcing and crowdfunding, and they may set up institutional budgets dedicated to taking on innovation projects. Leaders will be truly instrumental in igniting innovation in such organizations.

In general, as the leadership matures for innovation, we should see increasing connections between what is important to the organization (goals) and what is important to innovation. Therefore, maturity with respect to leadership should address the following questions:

- Role models: Are leaders posing as role models for innovation and participating in organization-wide innovation drives? Do they set an example by involving themselves in innovation projects?
- Innovation performance: Do leaders review innovation performance regularly, especially if financial returns are a critical factor for the organization? Although innovation should have a financial return, there may be some projects that have indirect impacts; in these cases, leaders should be able to demonstrate their importance.
- Leader support: The role of participation in hosting and sponsoring events related to creativity within an organization indicates a level of commitment to and backing of innovation. Leaders may create many such provisions for their organization. Are leaders' support and commitment evident?
- Strategic direction: Another indicator of how seriously leaders are taking an innovation challenge is the action that they take in planning and deploying the strategy for innovation as well as the role they play in providing strategic directives to improve innovation performance. Are innovation strategies and processes with targets clearly defined in the organization?
- Institute leadership and lower levels: To what extent does the organization have managers who truly encourage their team to participate in co-creation?
- Networking and partnerships: Does the organization demonstrate the constant flow of information through multiple communication channels? Do they create opportunity for networking internally and externally and build partnerships for innovation?

A scoresheet that can be used to analyze the leadership enabler appears in Table 4.1.

Leadership can score a maximum of forty points, which indicates a mature state of the organization in its innovation deployment. The leadership lever can be conceptualized as shown in Table 4.2 pertaining to the three stages of maturity based on the scores.

4.3.2 Component 2: People

The second component of the maturity model is the people. When we think of the people in the organization, we must consider them as innovative minds rather than simply people. When we acknowledge our people as creative minds, we truly appreciate their value as creative assets.

As we saw in Chap. 3, people can have a huge positive or negative effect on innovation. In innovative organizations, people are tied to innovation success. If people are not engaged, involved, and generating good ideas that they see through to execution, there will be no perfect innovation that will make an organization shine. As with the leadership component, there are many elements that go into nurturing, developing, and managing a pipeline of high-quality ideas. First, there need to be profitable ideas that result in financial benefit or in commercialization. Therefore, the people element of the innovation component must be nurtured well. An assessment of this component cautiously examines the alignment of people for innovation.

Predictably, as the organization matures and has more experience with innovation projects, it will see greater success in this category. Another important aspect to examine is how people are selected, trained, and leveraged to achieve the maximum benefit. Some of these may involve the use of appropriate tools, making tool rigor an important aspect. For example, people may need training for innovation. This training may be tool-specific, and the rigor of tool training provided may also impact training outcomes. As such, some key aspects are whether training is provided using the right tools and whether the right trainings are chosen for innovation elevation.

Specifically, the people element should be examined to understand the desire of employees to participate as well as their expertise and training. The examination should also include whether the organization is building employee motivation and offering opportunities for collective imagination. This entails asking the following questions:

- Desire for participation and involvement: The first target to ascertain is the level of involvement and engagement of the people. How is the organization ensuring its people's involvement and engagement? Are employees empowered to test their creativity? Do employees perceive the organization as being conducive for innovation? A more positive perception is better for innovation.
- Expertise: Does the organization have talented and experienced employees who can innovate? Are high-value innovations elicited from experienced employees?
- Training: This element helps to understand how well an organization is preparing its employees to innovate. Although organizational leaders have realized the power of innovation training and seen benefits reaped by highly innovative organizations, the training aspect is shallow in many organizations. It is often mixed with function-specific trainings or standard training programs without investing much on the infrastructure or providing the needed support to practice skills. At the initial stage, the key questions are: How does the organization analyze and build the expertise of its people? Does the organization provide training to its employees? At the advanced level, the diagnostic tool must focus on understanding the training rigor. Is there training rigor demonstrated? If tools are applied, what is the extent to which these tools are capable of creating the needed impact? As the organization matures, it becomes more important to have a highly sophisticated training system so that employees can understand all elements of creativity and innovation. With proper exposure, inexperienced organizations become aware of the importance of the right training, and they may tailor those trainings to their needs. For example, a company that we consulted for innovation had presented a number of trainings that employees were encouraged to attend, and these were implemented through a well-established yearly training calendar. Budgets were

allocated, and everything seemed to be perfect when it came to employee training. However, going through the depth of the program and organizational requirements, we identified a huge gap between what the organization actually needed and what was being delivered. The trainings did not aim at innovation outcomes. Another important aspect to consider in the training element is the improvement of learning and acceleration of benefits. While examining this element, we should ask: Who is trained in what? What kind of post-training support is offered? How is training leveraged in the long run?
- Teamwork: Are team rewards established? Do teams offer high-value innovations?
- Reward system: What does an organization do to motivate its employees? Are these rewards and recognitions fully appreciated by the employees? In matured organizations, rewards are fairly calculated as per their savings through established special annual award categories, and a transparent reward process is apparent.

There are different approaches to people management and many deployment positions, too. Each of these people elements may show a varied level of deployment; however, as the organization matures, most indicators are fully visible and are highly structured, showing a clear linkage to innovation success.

Johnson & Johansson is one company that exposes employees to outside influences and ideas through attendance at conferences, membership in professional societies, and similar activities to help break down insularity. The organization believes that employees' involvement in such areas can be measured and rewarded, if not monetarily, then through recognition and corporate support.

The overall score for people enablers is forty as shown in Table 4.3. When an organization achieves this score, its people enabler indicates a very strong positioning for innovation. However, an organization can target its maturity gradually and scores shown in Table 4.4 help to determine this maturity.

Table 4.3 Scoresheet for people component

Enabler indicators	Associated practices	Score
Desire for participation and involvement	Employees are actively involved in problem-solving and decision-making	1
	Employees contribute frequently to an idea management system	2
	Employees take responsibility to test and build prototypes	2
	The organization is able to maintain a consistent pipeline of ideas and implementations	2
Expertise	The organization has talented and experienced employees who can innovate	2
	The organization transfers knowledge, skills, and ideas across departments in an organized way	2
Training	High-value innovations are elicited from experienced employees	2
	Innovation-related trainings are a regular feature	1
	Training tools are chosen for their rigor and being appropriate to innovation goals	2
Building employee motivation	Employees perceive the organization as being conducive to innovation	3
	Employees enjoy their job tasks with a degree of freedom and flexibility	2
	Employees' work structure provides them with opportunities to improve their tasks	2
	Employees can seek/receive support to work on their ideas	2
	Work life features happiness, challenging jobs, work complexity, employee well-being, autonomy, and coworker support	2
	Employees are encouraged to engage in informed risk-taking	2
Opportunities for collective imagination	Team rewards are established	1
	Teams offer high-value innovations	2
	Employees from all levels are encouraged to participate	2
	Collaboration and knowledge-sharing are encouraged	2
	Every employee is aware that innovation is important	1
	Open systems to collaborate and exchange ideas are established	3
Total score		40

Table 4.4 Maturity table for people component

Score	Maturity level
<18	Initial
Between 18 and 34	Developmental
Above 34	Advanced

4.3.3 Component 3: Capability-Building

The third component is capability-building. Organizations need to engage in innovation capability-building centered around processes, people, resources, and places. A highly design-oriented innovation organization such as IBM also uses a 3P approach to create a culture of innovation. A 3P approach emphasizes people, practices, and places. In our assessment model, we also emphasize other capabilities, such as strategy, resource mobilization, setting up rewards, and offering recognition.

Overall, capability-building is an important aspect for creating a deep-rooted culture of innovation in an organization. This component builds a solid foundation to spur innovation in an organization. Each element of capability-building must be nurtured to achieve superior results. Resources here mainly focus on establishing appropriate financial support in the form of putting together budgets for innovations or other infrastructure-related expenditures necessary for innovations to occur. This may also include technology enhancements or new partnership acquisition. The process component requires organizations to establish processes to support innovation and invest in building collaborative places for employees to come together to engage in idea exchanges and discussions or to propose new solutions.

A very important aspect that can promote innovation is the availability of the right infrastructure to transform ideas into actionable solutions that eventually result in bringing financial value to the organization. Indeed, this requires the interaction of people, technology, processes, and resources. In this vein, the places component refers to hubs that enable the right interaction of such elements. For example, in an innovation organization, this is leveraged through creating places such as collaborative workrooms, innovation labs, or even virtual spaces for creative minds to freely engage in high-quality thinking. At the same time, organizations can remain in limbo or kill creativity if they do not shed their rigid traditional approaches. Assessing such elements requires scrutinizing to what extent these elements are leveraged. However, in each of these elements, the deployment levels will vary, as we will discuss in reference to each:

- Resources: Most organizations mobilize financial budgets, technology enhancements, and physical resources, as necessary, for innovation. At the initial stage, the internal management of funding may be organized, but external fundraising options may not be considered. Technology enhancement may not be highly sophisticated and may take place in a staggered manner while resource allocation may occur only after the pilot run of a project. At the developmental stage, funding may follow a systematic budgeting process, and a high level of fund management may be visible, showing some readiness to access external funding. A fully innovative firm at the advanced stage would have established a systematic process for budget allocation and fully provisioned for crowdfunding or have a pool of options to mobilize the financial, technical, or related resources. Such an organization does not abandon the process as a result of failing to meet its resource needs. Financial resources may be limited initially, but additional management support to gather resources as required may be possible as the organization matures. Mature deployments, therefore, evidence innovative ways of gathering the resources for innovation. The assessment of this element should address the following question: To what extent are resources integrated or gathered within the organization in support of innovation?
- Process: A little can go a long way in the innovation process. Although it is more concerned with the administrative aspect of the innovation process, the process element helps an organization to establish its position for innovation to begin. When an organization molds an innovation culture by establishing processes to manage innovation, this approach can go a long way toward sustaining momentum. To encourage innovation, people in the organization must be aware of the processes that are in place that enable them to be innovative. Innovative organizations at the grassroots level will demonstrate the establishment of such processes but may lack a full deployment because their

effectiveness may be at basic levels. As the organization matures, innovation processes are fully capable of demonstrating their effectiveness. Moreover, the problem does not lie in a lack of ideas, but more in the successful management of the innovation process from an idea to the final product. The reality is that the most innovative companies such Apple, P&G's, or Toyota achieve their successes because they follow a disciplined innovation process, and the best way for a firm to become an innovator is to adopt a systematic approach that helps manage the large scale risks and opportunities that an organization faces (Morris 2011).

- Places: This element determines how well an organization is prepared to equip its people by leveraging innovation places/locations. Innovation places are innovation hubs, creativity rooms, or facilities that are built to encourage brainstorming. Some organizations have become enthusiastic about establishing innovation labs that are necessary for large-scale innovation to take place. In the early stages, such spaces may be limited or may be under negotiation or discussion. Eventually, organizations create these dedicated places as innovation matures, and may even outsource their labs for collaborations. For example, J&J employs a full range of innovation vehicles, especially early on in the development chain. Each vehicle is suited to a particular stage and a specific goal: incubators for young ideas, and innovation labs for companies that are looking to mature.
- Practices: There are many important innovation-friendly practices that organizations should nurture; without these, organizations will struggle to obtain good innovation results. As important as other elements of capability-building, good organizational practices are key to generating high-quality ideas. The organization's structure, authority, communication mechanisms, and support systems should be in place. First, clear guidelines, awareness of innovation, and a supportive organizational culture should begin to take shape. This development is likely to mature as targets are set and performances are reviewed. Eventually, organizations begin to celebrate their success and introduce a number of creativity-stimulation workshops, and it becomes an organization-wide activity where support for cross-functions and idea-

exchanges can go beyond their functional lines. More team-based initiatives come into existence, and innovations are centrally handled rather than being limited to certain departments. Moreover, an organization should put ideas into practice, particularly because the mobilization of resources for pilot testing is needed once an idea is received. Managers are also responsible for reviewing, evaluating, and providing necessary feedback and support in improving the initial ideas and taking them to the next stage. The mechanics for constant revaluation and feedback should be a key aspect around the innovation practices of the organization. Maintaining a practice of having dedicated roles and structures to handle innovation is a good example. Organograms of innovative organizations now feature positions such as "innovation executive" at different levels of the organization. Typically, as in the case of all other elements, the deployment and maturity of practices will differ; hence, assessment should scrutinize the extent to which organizations are prepared to put in place innovation management practices and how these help organizations to leverage the benefit.

- Strategy: Highly innovative organizations get things right from the beginning through a well-established strategy. Leaders carry the responsibility to guide and direct employees toward innovation in order to strengthen the organization's competitive advantage. However, at an initial stage, the strategy may be established, but the action plans may not be fully integrated into individual routines. While establishing a well-developed strategy is an important first step, organizations at the developmental stage should be able to provide good evidence of the strategy being integrated and assessed. In highly innovative organizations, this is well structured, outcomes are measured, and strategy assessment and refinements are visible.
- Rewards and recognition: In order to fully engage and motivate its employees, the organization must establish rewards and recognitions. Leadership should be fully engaged in this process of establishing rewards and ensure the organization sets aside the needed budget. While there may be simple schemes in the initial stages, a robust and lucrative scheme comes into the picture as the organization matures.

The assessment of this enabler should follow Table 4.5:

The overall score for organizational capability component is fifty-five as shown in Table 4.5. The capability development lever can be conceptualized as shown in Table 4.6 pertaining to the three stages of maturity based on the scores.

4.3.4 Component 4: Innovation Outcomes

The final component of the model is innovation outcomes, which signify the benefits achieved through innovation. The focus of this framework is to assess the outcomes as well as the outputs. Outputs are typically the immediate results of a process, such as the number of ideas generated or the number of projects completed. While these results indeed form the basis for outcomes, the actual focus of innovation should be on the *process* of achieving the *outcomes*. Outcomes, conversely, represent the broader spectrum of impacts resulting in business sustainability, stakeholder satisfaction, and the extent to which organizations deliver quality products through their improved processes. The process ensures the longevity and sustainability of the efforts. Overall, the model assesses the achievement of both sides (i.e. the process and the outcomes), which forms a strong basis for innovation success.

In general, when we talk about outcomes, a typical assessment should answer questions such as: Where is the impact created? What is the outcome achieved?

As El Bassiti and Ajhoun (2016) explained, outcomes can fall into any of these categories: (1) new products, such as assistive technologies for mobile phones; (2) new services, such as mobile banking; (3) new processes, such as continuous improvement methods and crowdsourcing; (4) new organizational forms, such as community interest companies or networks; and (5) new business models, such as social franchising or just-in-time models applied to social needs. All these outputs result in outcomes such as profitability or the creation of generic social impact as well, although specific social innovations generally result in more substantial social impacts. For example, the OECD's (2015) Better Life Index helps organizations target impact in one of these eleven indicators in terms of a university context:

Table 4.5 Scoresheet for capability building component

Enabler indicator	Associated practices	Score
Resources	Internal budgets are established	1
	There are multiple arrangements to seek external funding when needed	3
	Technology enhancements are visible	2
	Highly sophisticated environments are in place	2
	Technology is regularly being updated/purchased	3
	It is easy to seek and obtain resources as needed	3
	Resource allocation takes time	2
Process	The organization has a process established to oversee innovation	2
	The innovation process is highly effective from idea selection to deployment	2
	Effective evaluations criteria are in place	2
	Ideas are managed centrally	1
	Timely feedback is given on ideas, and encouragement is offered for prototyping or further development	1
Places	Meagre meeting rooms are available for collaboration	1
	The organization has innovation hubs, creativity rooms, or facilities that are built for brainstorming	3
	Facilities are used by external sources	3
	The organization can also use innovation hubs outside the organization	2
	Has facilities of incubators for early innovators	1
Practices	Effective policies are in place to support innovation	1
	An innovation department is established on the organogram	2
	Organization has a culture that is aware of innovation awareness	1
	The organization's organogram features positions such as "innovation executive"	2
Strategy	An innovation strategy is established	3
	Strategy and action plans are well integrated and operationalized	3
	Strategy is assessed and refined as needed	3
Rewards and recognition	The organization has established reward and recognition schemes	1
	Schemes are proportionate to the benefit accrued from the implementation	2
	Rewards are highly competitive	2
	Leaders themselves ensure the recognition and motivation of employees	2
Total score		55

Table 4.6 Maturity table for organizational capability component

Score	Maturity level
<25	Initial
Between 25 and 40	Developmental
Above 40	Advanced

- housing (rooms per person and dwellings with basic facilities, housing expenditure);
- jobs (employment rate, long-term unemployment rate, job security);
- education (years in education, educational attainment, students' skills);
- civic engagement (voter turnout, consultation on rulemaking);
- life satisfaction;
- work–life balance (employees working long hours, time devoted to leisure and personal care);
- income (household net-adjusted disposable income and household financial wealth);
- community (social support network);
- environment (air pollution, water quality);
- health (life expectancy, self-reported health); and
- safety (assault rate, homicide rate).

The next aspect would analyze questions such as: How is innovation being achieved? In this context, we oversee process-related outcomes. How effective is the process? How does the process ensure sustainable results? In doing so, we aim at understanding whether the organization is able to achieve the following aspects:

- Profitability: What revenue is generated as a result of innovation?
- Product quality: To what extent is product quality enhanced through the ideas implemented?
- Process improvements: To what extent has the process been enhanced to achieve superior results?
- Stakeholder satisfaction: To what extent are customers happy with the innovative products and services produced by the organization? To

what extent do employees agree to achieve the overall goal of the organization in terms of innovation and the impact created on society?

- Innovation portfolio: To what extent is the organization generating and managing the innovation pipeline to sustain innovation?

A score sheet to assess this complement is presented in Table 4.7.

Assessment of each of the elements of 4C component model at the initial stage may reveal the results of one or more elements, but not all elements of innovation outcomes would be visible in an organization during this stage. However, the organization's innovation portfolio would offer evidence of ideas being collected, prototyped, and resulting in new or improved services or products. At the same time, some evidence of improvements in processes may also be visible.

At the developmental stage, organizations may be able to showcase a few successful innovation projects and demonstrate how the innovation portfolio is shaping up with notable revenues or profits. The organization at the developmental stage can also illustrate product quality as well as improvements in processes. As a result, the organization should also be able to showcase results in terms of stakeholder (e.g. customer or employee) satisfaction.

At the advanced stage, the organization should have a good innovation portfolio that shows a steady stream of innovation projects and profits earned with distinguished new and improved services or products. Such an organization is clearly able to achieve its process enhancement and has collected several pieces of evidence of stakeholder satisfaction, and they feed into their process of innovation clearly.

Overall, the outcomes of the innovation should address these questions:

- Can the organization clearly demonstrate the profits earned from its innovations?
- Is there an innovation portfolio to showcase a number of new services or products being introduced?
- Is there evidence to showcase the improvements made in terms of existing processes?

Table 4.7 Scoresheet for innovation outcomes

Innovation outcome	Associated practices	Score
Profits	Innovation revenue is significant and consistent	2
	There are new segments or sectors increased due to new product or services	2
	Segments or sectors increased due to new products or services are increased regularly	3
New product/service development and enhancement	New product and service development is rare and not consistent	1
	New product and service development is significant and consistent	3
	New product and service development is significant, consistent, and the organization is able to increase services or products to meet the growth challenge	3
	The organization is able to demonstrate customer co-development and experience	2
	The organization is able to demonstrate highly consistent and significant customer co-development and experience	3
Process enhancements	Process enhancements are rare and not consistent	1
	Process enhancements are significant and consistent	3
	The organization is able to return to market rapidly with improvements	3
	The organization is able to return to market at moderate speed	2
	The organization's return time to market is very slow	2
	Innovation clearly has some process outcomes, cycle time, and error reduction	3
	Cost-saving is achieved due to innovation efforts	3
	Process enhancements are significant, consistent, and show a positive trend	3
Innovation capability and portfolio	The organization has a significant number of projects	2
	The organization is able to increase projects significantly and consistently	2
	Organizational capabilities are under development	2
	The firm has well-developed organizational capabilities	2
	The cost of abandoned projects is high	1
	There are abandoned innovation products	2
	Capital investment is made for innovation activities	3
	Innovation targets the local community and creates social impacts	3
	The organization has educated and capable people as innovators	3
	The organization has dedicated budgets for innovation or funding options are in place	3
	The firm has highly commendable organizational capabilities that are sustainable	3
Total score		65

Table 4.8 Maturity table for innovation outcomes

Score	Maturity level
<35	Initial
Between 35 and 55	Developmental
Above 55	Advanced

- Is there evidence of improved service or product quality of existing services or products?
- Is there evidence of designing the products or services with customer involvement (customer co-creation)?
- How does the organization know whether its products are well aligned as a result of active customer engagement or co-creation? Does the organization have any results indicating these?
- How do stakeholders such as people or society at large appreciate the organization's services and products? Do stakeholders feel these services and products meet their requirements and have impact on their lives?

The innovation outcome can be conceptualized as shown in Table 4.8 pertaining to the three stages of maturity based on the scores.

4.3.5 Overall Assessment

The assessment table can be used to ascertain a score for innovation outcomes as shown in Table 4.9.

The model provides a possible score of 200 in total. If an organization achieves this score, it is in good standing.

So, our next key question is: How do we apply the assessment tool to ascertain the scores?

4.4 How to Use the CIAM Tool

The assessment involves a three-step process of planning, carrying out, and closing the assessment. Each step provides input for the next stage. The following guidelines are to be used to assess and interpret the organization's innovation maturity.

Table 4.9 Assessment framework

Enabler indicators	Associated practices	Score
Leadership	Leaders act as role models	3
	Leaders institute leadership throughout the organization	3
	Leaders provide strategic directions and measure innovation performance	2
	Leaders consistently allocate the resources needed to fund staff innovation efforts	2
	Leaders support, empower, and develop their employees to engage them in problem-solving	3
Communication and networking	Leaders focus communication aspects of the organization to create maximum opportunities for employees to collaborate freely along horizontal and vertical axes and increase the opportunity for team-ups	2
	Leaders create communication opportunities and facilitate internal and external networking, driving toward high-quality exchanges between various elements of the organization	2
Relational creation/co-creation	Leaders are engaged in building a relationship of co-creation among employees	2
	Few boundaries exist in leveraging their people to network, build internal or external partnerships, take initiative, and engage in decision-making processes at large	3
	Leaders ensure co-development with customers	3
Mobilize support	Leaders may have created partnerships and networks to leverage their innovation potential	2
	Leaders use several collaborative opportunities such as crowdsourcing and crowdfunding, and they set up institutional budgets dedicated to taking on innovation projects	3
	Leaders support and create events to increase creativity or facilitate relevant trainings	3
Subtotal		40

(*continued*)

Table 4.9 (continued)

Enabler indicators	Associated practices	Score
Desire for participation and Involvement	Employees are actively involved in problem-solving and decision-making	1
	Employees contribute frequently to an idea management system	1
	Employees take responsibility to test and build prototypes	1
	The organization is able to maintain a consistent pipeline of ideas and implementations	1
Expertise	The organization has talented and experienced employees who can innovate	2
	The organization transfers knowledge, skills, and ideas across departments in an organized way	2
Training	High-value innovations are elicited from experienced employees	1
	Innovation-related trainings are a regular feature	2
	Training tools are chosen for their rigor and being appropriate to innovation goals	2
Building employee motivation	Employees perceive the organization as being conducive to innovation	1
	Employees enjoy their job tasks with a degree of freedom and flexibility	1
	Employees' work structure provides them with opportunities to improve their tasks	1
	Employees can seek/receive support to work on their ideas	1
	Work–life features happiness, challenging jobs, work complexity, employee well-being, autonomy, and coworker support	2 2
	Employees are encouraged to engage in informed risk-taking	
Opportunities for collective imagination	Team rewards are established	1
	Teams offer high-value innovations	2
	Employees from all levels are encouraged to participate	1
	Collaboration and knowledge-sharing are encouraged	1
	Every employee is aware that innovation is important	1
	Open systems to collaborate and exchange ideas are established	3
Subtotal		40

(continued)

Table 4.9 (continued)

Enabler indicators	Associated practices	Score
Resources	Internal budgets are established	1
	There are multiple arrangements to seek external funding when needed	3
	Technology enhancements are visible	1
	Highly sophisticated environments are in place	3
	Technology is regularly being updated/purchased	2
	It is easy to seek and obtain resources as needed	1
	Resource allocation takes time	1
Process	The organization has a process established to oversee innovation	1
	The innovation process is highly effective	2
	Effective evaluations criteria are in place	2
	Ideas are managed centrally	1
	Timely feedback is given on ideas, and encouragement is offered for prototyping or further development	2
Places	Meagre meeting rooms are available for collaboration	1
	The organization has innovation hubs, creativity rooms, or facilities that are built for brainstorming	3
	Facilities are used by external sources	3
	The organization can also use innovation hubs outside the organization	2
Practices	Effective policies are in place to support innovation	1
	An innovation department is established on the organogram	2
	The organization has a culture that is aware of innovation	1
	The organization's organogram features positions such as "innovation executive"	1
Strategy	A strategy is established	1
	Strategy and action plans are well integrated and operationalized	2
	Strategy is assessed and refined as needed	3
Rewards and recognition	The organization has established reward and recognition schemes	1
	Schemes are proportionate to the benefit accrued from the implementation	2
	Rewards are highly competitive	2
	Leaders themselves ensure the recognition and motivation of employees	2
Subtotal		55

(*continued*)

Table 4.9 (continued)

Innovation outcome	Associated practices	Score
Profits	Innovation revenue is significant and consistent	2
	There are new segments or sectors increased due to new product or services	2
	Segments or sectors increased due to new products or services are increased regularly	3
New product/service development and enhancement	New product and service development is rare and not consistent	1
	New product and service development is significant and consistent	2
	New product and service development is significant, consistent, and the organization is able to increase services or products to meet the growth challenge	3
	The organization is able to demonstrate customer co-development and experience	2
	The organization is able to demonstrate highly consistent and significant customer co-development and experience	3
Process enhancements	Process enhancements are rare and not consistent	1
	Process enhancements are significant and consistent	2
	The organization is able to return to market rapidly with improvements	3
	The organization is able to return to market at moderate speed	2
	The organization's return time to market is very slow	1
	Innovation clearly has some process outcomes, cycle time, and error reduction	2
	Cost-saving is achieved due to innovation efforts	2
	Process enhancements are significant, consistent, and show a positive trend	3

(continued)

Table 4.9 (continued)

Innovation outcome	Associated practices	Score
Innovation capability and portfolio	The organization has a significant number of projects	1
	The organization is able to increase projects significantly and consistently	2
	Organizational capabilities are under development	1
	The firm has well-developed organizational capabilities	2
	The cost of abandoned projects is high	1
	There are abandoned innovation products	2
	Capital investment is made for innovation activities	3
	Innovation targets the local community and creates social impacts	3
	The organization has educated and capable people as innovators	3
	The organization has dedicated budgets for innovation or funding options are in place	3
	The firm has highly commendable organizational capabilities that are sustainable	3
Subtotal		65
Total score		200

1. Planning: Organizations should form a team to carry out the assessments. The team should involve members of each key area who have adequate knowledge and understanding of the operations and overall system of the organization and carry out their data collection.

2. Upon completion, the assessors should analyze the data and prepare the scoresheet for each of the components 4C models as shown in Table 4.10. The total scores achieved should be analyzed using the maturity in Table 4.10.

An overall score of less than seventy-five indicates that innovation deployment is in the initial stage. A score of more than 75–165 indicates the developmental stage, and more than 165 indicates the advanced stage. Indicators that fall in the initial stage or exhibit no evidence should

Table 4.10 Maturity scores

Score	Initial
0–75	Initial level
75–165	Developmental level
>165	Advanced level

be identified for improvement. The organization's improvement roadmap should be developed by choosing possible solutions shown under the developmental stage. This exercise should be repeated for indicators marked in the developmental stage as well. In this case, the improvement roadmap should propose solutions shown under the advanced stage.

Once the template is completed, add each enabler score and securitize the score against the following five key questions.

4.5 Measuring Progress and Success Using the CIAM Tool

The application of the above framework will provide insights for understanding:

- Do we have the right pieces in place?
- Is anything missing?
- What are we doing well?
- What are our challenges?
- What is most important for us to work on next?

4.5.1 Do We Have the Right Pieces in Place?

The answer to this question indicates whether the triggers of innovation exist in the organization. If so, to what extent are they existent? These answers, for example, determine whether leadership, people, and capability-building are embedded into the system and whether their level of existence is visible. In this sense, the organization should be able to achieve a minimum score of 200, which would indicate the existence of each enabler.

A score of up to fifteen indicates the initial level of leadership, while thirty-five and above indicates that leadership is at the advanced stage, and a higher score indicates good status leadership lever.

A score of up to fifteen indicates the initial level of the people enabler, while thirty and above indicates that the people lever is at the advanced stage, and a higher score indicates good status people lever.

A score of twenty-five indicates the initial level of capability-building, forty-five and above indicates the capability-building lever is at the advanced stage, and a higher score indicates good status capability-building lever.

A score of thirty indicates the initial level of innovation outcomes, while fifty and above indicates the innovation outcomes are at the advanced stage, and a higher score indicates good status for innovation outcomes.

4.5.2 Is Anything Missing?

The next level of analysis should be to determine whether anything is missing in the system. In particular, organizations should pay attention to the factors that show a low level of maturity. Factors and elements that have a value of less than ten are to be clear points for the organization's next actions.

Organizations may exhibit evidence of a high level in various factors but lack evidence of fostering some associated elements. For example, organizations often have leaders who are true role models and may be committed, but who fail to reinforce co-creation. The system may fail to leverage middle management co-working environments, and this oversight may drift down to traditional management models. Under such systems, the pressure will build to work according to deadlines, leaving little opportunity to reinforce innovation.

4.5.3 What Are We Doing Well?

Going deeper into the analysis, the next level of discussion should revolve around analyzing what the organization is good at. Learning from an organization's own good practices is the key to success and sustainable results. Enablers that are at an advanced level indicate that the organization is doing well in these areas. An action plan to replicate these good practices can then be devised to pull the other levers.

4.5.4 What Are Our Challenges?

Now it is time to ponder the organization's challenges in relation to each of the model's factors. Brainstorming questions should include: Why do we have the results that we have? What are our challenges in ascertaining these triggers of innovation? Deep questioning such as this may enable the organization to foresee the challenges that must be addressed either internally or externally. For example, an organization with visible innovation strategies and processes but ineffective deployment faces a challenge because employees are not well prepared to take advantage of the innovation infrastructure in place. This deficiency may need to be addressed by asking: Why has this been so? What actions are to be taken to resolve this challenge? A deep investigation into such challenges can help to draw a map of interventions that should be taken to better leverage each enabler.

4.5.5 What Is Most Important for Us to Work on Next?

Having a wide picture of the entire organization should help leadership narrow down those important aspects that need working on. It is important at this stage to understand the relevance and interconnections between the results.

4.6 Defining the Path to Success

Assessment plays a key role in helping the organization define its new path to success. A detailed analysis based on the above scrutiny of key questions highlights the strong and weak areas of innovation-enabling elements of the organization. Leaderships and teams then have a responsibility to redraw the goals and objectives of their innovation and outline a realistic plan to consider in a given timeframe.

Here is an example of an organization showcasing an analysis of the assessment results shown in Table 4.11.

As we can see from Table 4.11, this organization's leadership is strong while its people and capability-building scored lower. In terms of people, the organization has scored low in this category in general. This indicates that the organization will need to pull out its levers for the practices aspect as well. Similarly, the capability-building component has scored fairly well, which indicates that the organization is almost at a balanced level with leadership and organizational capability-building. However, it has not created innovation-fostering practices, and it may have structures that are hindering the drive for innovation. Hence, some of the actions that could be recommended are as follows:

1. Create a new organogram with innovation in mind, adding positions and policies to boost the innovation drive.
2. Restructure or build incentives or a rewards model to boost ideas.
3. Establish a good evaluation scheme to move ideas to the next stage of development.
4. Recognize teamwork and create team structures.
5. Empower the co-creation culture.

Overall, the organization received a moderate score because it has a certain level of leadership and organizational capability-building in place. There is substantial scope to improve the organization's standing by boosting the people enabler and even leveraging the other two enablers to the next stage of maturity.

Table 4.11 Example assessment

Enabler indicators	Associated practices	Max score	Our score
Leadership	Leaders act as role models	3	0
	Leaders institute leadership throughout the organization	3	2
	Leaders provide strategic directions and measure innovation performance	2	2
	Leaders consistently allocate the resources needed to fund staff innovation efforts	2	2
	Leaders support, empower, and develop their employees to engage them in problem-solving	3	2
Communication and networking	Leaders focus communication aspects of the organization to create maximum opportunities for employees to collaborate freely along horizontal and vertical axes and increase the opportunity for team-ups	2	2
	Leaders create communication opportunities and facilitate internal and external networking, driving toward high-quality exchanges between various elements of the organization	2	2
Relational creation/co-creation	Leaders are engaged in building a relationship of co-creation among employees	2	1
	Few boundaries exist in leveraging their people to network, build internal or external partnerships, take initiative, and engage in decision-making processes at large	3	2
	Leaders ensure co-development with customers	3	0
Mobilize support	Leaders may have created partnerships and networks to leverage their innovation potential	1	2
	Leaders use several collaborative opportunities such as crowdsourcing and crowdfunding, and they set up institutional budgets dedicated to taking on innovation projects	2	2
	Leaders support and create events to increase creativity or facilitate relevant trainings	2	2
Subtotal		40	21

(*continued*)

Table 4.11 (continued)

Enabler indicators	Associated practices	Score	
Desire for participation and Involvement	Employees are actively involved in problem-solving and decision-making	1	1
	Employees contribute frequently to an idea management system	1	1
	Employees take responsibility to test and build prototypes	1	1
	The organization is able to maintain a consistent pipeline of ideas and implementations	1	0
Expertise	The organization has talented and experienced employees who can innovate	2	1
	The organization transfers knowledge, skills, and ideas across departments in an organized way	2	1
Training	High-value innovations are elicited from experienced employees	1	1
	Innovation-related trainings are a regular feature	2	0
	Training tools are chosen for their rigor and being appropriate to innovation goals	2	0
Building employee motivation	Employees perceive the organization as being conducive to innovation	1	0
	Employees enjoy their job tasks with a degree of freedom and flexibility	1	0
	Employees' work structure provides them with opportunities to improve their tasks	1	0
	Employees can seek/receive support to work on their ideas	1	0
	Work–life features happiness, challenging jobs, work complexity, employee well-being, autonomy, and coworker support	2	0
	Employees are encouraged to engage in informed risk-taking	2	
Opportunities for collective imagination	Team rewards are established	1	1
	Teams offer high-value innovations	2	0
	Employees from all levels are encouraged to participate	1	0
	Collaboration and knowledge-sharing are encouraged	1	0
	Every employee is aware that innovation is important	1	1
	Open systems to collaborate and exchange ideas are established	3	1
Subtotal		40	10

(*continued*)

Table 4.11 (continued)

Enabler indicators	Associated practices	Score	
Resources	Internal budgets are established	1	1
	There are multiple arrangements to seek external funding when needed	3	2
	Technology enhancements are visible	1	2
	Highly sophisticated environments are in place	3	1
	Technology is regularly being updated/ purchased	2	1
	It is easy to seek and obtain resources as needed	1	1
	Resource allocation takes time	1	1
Process	The organization has a process established to oversee innovation	1	1
	The innovation process is highly effective	2	1
	Effective evaluations criteria are in place	2	1
	Ideas are managed centrally	1	1
	Timely feedback is given on ideas, and encouragement is offered for prototyping or further development	2	1
Places	Mere meeting rooms are available for collaboration	1	1
	The organization has innovation hubs, creativity rooms, or facilities that are built for brainstorming	3	1
	Facilities are used by external sources	3	1
	The organization can also use innovation hubs outside the organization	2	1
Practices	Effective policies are in place to support innovation	1	1
	An innovation department is established on the organogram	2	1
	Innovation awareness	1	1
	The organization's organogram features positions such as "innovation executive"	1	1
Strategy	A strategy is established	1	1
	Strategy and action plans are well integrated and operationalized	2	
	Strategy is assessed and refined as needed	3	1
Rewards and recognition	The organization has established reward and recognition schemes	1	1
	Schemes are proportionate to the benefit accrued from the implementation	2	1
	Rewards are highly competitive	2	1
	Leaders themselves ensure the recognition and motivation of employees	2	1
Subtotal		55	28

(*continued*)

Table 4.11 (continued)

Innovation outcome	Associated practices	Score	
	Innovation revenue is significant and consistent	2	1
	There are new segments or sectors increased due to new product or services	2	1
	Segments or sectors increased due to new products or services are increased regularly	3	1
New product/service development and enhancement	New product and service development is rare and not consistent	1	1
	New product and service development is significant and consistent	2	1
	New product and service development is significant, consistent, and the organization is able to increase services or products to meet the growth challenge	3	1
	The organization is able to demonstrate customer co-development and experience	2	1
	The organization is able to demonstrate highly consistent and significant customer co-development and experience	3	1
Process enhancements	Process enhancements are rare and not consistent	1	1
	Process enhancements are significant and consistent	2	2
	The organization is able to return to market rapidly with improvements	3	1
	The organization is able to return to market at moderate speed	2	1
	The organization's return time to market is very slow	1	1
	Innovation clearly has some process outcomes, cycle time, and error reduction	2	1
	Cost-saving is achieved due to innovation efforts	2	1
	Process enhancements are significant, consistent, and show a positive trend	3	1
Innovation capability and portfolio	The organization has a significant number of projects	1	0
	The organization is able to increase projects significantly and consistently	2	1
	Organizational capabilities are under development	1	1
	The firm has well-developed organizational capabilities	2	1
	The cost of abandoned projects is high	1	1

(continued)

Table 4.11 (continued)

Innovation outcome	Associated practices	Score	
	There are abandoned innovation products	2	1
	Capital investment is made for innovation activities	3	1
	Innovation targets the local community and creates social impacts	3	1
	The organization has educated and capable people as innovators	3	1
	The organization has dedicated budgets for innovation or funding options are in place	3	1
	The firm has highly commendable organizational capabilities that are sustainable	3	1
Subtotal		65	27
Total score		200	90

4.7 Conclusion

This chapter illustrated how to use the CIAM tool to evaluate an organization's innovation stage based on the 4C Framework of Innovation Assessment. The initial assessment results should be analyzed from five key perspectives to get a deeper understanding of how the organization can develop its action plan to improve innovation components for a superior performance. Each component can achieve a maturity level from initial (level 1) to advanced (level 3), providing a complete picture of the organization's innovation journey. Maturity models are typically staged models providing a predefined roadmap for improvement based on proven grouping and moving from "initial" to "continuously improving" processes and associated practices. Each stage, called a "maturity level," has a set of practice areas that indicate where innovation actors should focus their improvement efforts. This gives an initial indicator for an organization to build its capability and nudge its performance toward the next level. A team with adequate knowledge of the organization should be formed to carry out the internal assessment. They should then help develop an action plan appropriate for the enhancement of each enabler.

It is critical to create a measurement model that provides a useful basis for managers to monitor and gauge innovation performance, detect faults, and identify repairs, in order to help the organization build its capacity to innovate systemically. In dynamic and sometimes chaotic organizations, employees need to have more than average competences to innovate (Cozijnsen and Vrakking 2013; Weick and Quinn 1999).

References

Adams, R., J. Bessant, and R. Phelps. 2006. Innovation Management Measurement: A Review. *International Journal of Management Reviews* 8 (1): 21–47.

Cozijnsen, A.J., and W.J. Vrakking. 2013. *Veranderkunde ("Change Management")*. Deventer: Kluwer.

El Bassiti, L., and R. Ajhoun. 2016. Towards Innovation Excellence: Why and How to Measure Innovation Performance? In *Information and Communication Technology for the Muslim World (ICT4M), 2016 6th International Conference*, pp. 99–104. IEEE.

Kerka, F., B. Kriegesmann, and M.G. Schwering. 2009. Evaluating Innovation Ideas: A Comprehensive Approach to New Product Development. *International Journal of Technology Intelligence and Planning* 5 (2): 118–137.

Morris, L. 2011. *The Innovation Master Plan: The CEO's Guide to Innovation*. Walnut Creek: Innovation Academy.

Muller, A., L. Välikangas, and P. Merlyn. 2005. Metrics for Innovation: Guidelines for Developing a Customized Suite of Innovation Metrics. *Strategy & Leadership* 33 (1): 37–45.

OECD. 2015. Better Life Index. http://www.oecdbetterlifeindex.org/. Accessed 8 Sept 2015.

Weick, K.E., and R.E. Quinn. 1999. Organizational Change and Development. *Annual Review of Psychology* 50 (1): 361–386.

5

Innovation in Action

5.1 Innovation Assessment and Awards

In this chapter, we will discuss two innovation assessments in UAE that are deployed to encourage organizations to embrace innovation. UAE innovation award launched in 2017 and American Society for Quality (ASQ) innovation award was launched in 2016. There are several other innovations related awards administered by UAE government which are illustrated in Chap. 1. The focus of this chapter is to assist organizations to action innovation within their organization and begin to embrace the change by showcasing the profiles of key winners of assessed using UAE innovation award and ASQ innovation award. The chapter also illustrates the assessments are awards in addition to giving the perspectives of the assessment leaders. Among global frameworks, for example in Canada an innovation award namely, Governor General's Innovation Awards has been established. The objectives of the Governor General's Innovation Awards are to celebrate excellence in innovation across all sectors of Canadian society, inspire Canadians, particularly Canadian youth, to be entrepreneurial innovators, and foster an active culture of innovation that has a meaningful impact on their lives (innovation.ca). Each year, up to

F. Lasrado, *Fostering Creativity and Innovation*,
https://doi.org/10.1007/978-3-319-99121-4_5

six award winners will be identified through a two-stage, merit-based selection process. This process is managed by the Canada Foundation for Innovation. Their aim is to have at least one young innovator among the winners who is thirty years of age or younger and who, individually or as leader of a team and/or organization, has been undertaking exceptional transformative and innovative activities. The program operates on an annual cycle, with an awards ceremony held each spring. The Office of the Secretary to the Governor General oversees the execution of all aspects of the program. In order to meet the objectives of inspiring Canadians and fostering a culture of entrepreneurial innovation, the awards program partners participate in communications and outreach activities. These activities will help build national awareness of the goals of the program and foster a culture of innovation in the country by celebrating the accomplishments of awards winners as broadly as possible. The Office of the Secretary to the Governor General oversees and coordinates the communications and outreach activities of core partner organizations.

On the other hand, Ideas America is an internationally recognized organization serving professional managers and administrators of employee ideas, involvement and innovation systems for seventy-five years by providing quality educational programs, publications, benchmarking and networking opportunities. Their members are leaders who are dedicated to building organizations that engage their employees, encouraging them to contribute to their organizations at many levels and in many ways. Ideas America annually recognizes the best ideas submitted from employees of its organizational members. Their international awards program is designed to recognize employee involvement professional and idea programs for their achievements. Similarly, in UAE there are other two awards which invite applications for innovation awards. These are discussed in the next section.

5.2 UAE Innovation Award

UAE Innovation Award to spread innovation culture throughout UAE private sector, has been launched and it covers a wide range of industries such as Health & Wellbeing, Education & Learning,

Energy & Utility, Technology & Communication, Transport, Social & Community Development, Retail & Consumer Goods, Financial Services, Heritage, Art & Culture, Sports & Recreation, Real Estate & Construction, Manufacturing, Tourism & Hospitality, and Professional Services, Marketing & Media, NGO & Non-Profit etc. The first Cycle of UAE Innovation Award was launched by Dubai Quality Group Board of Directors under the patronage of H.H. Sheikh Ahmed Bin Saeed Al Maktoum. The UAE Innovation Award is focusing on the private sector and it differs from other awards by its scope and objectives. The award framework and criteria have been designed based on world-class innovation concepts and best practices, and is be a great tool for companies to assess and raise their innovation maturity. By spreading innovation culture throughout the private sector, the UAE Innovation award will greatly contribute to the achievement of the national innovation strategy aimed at making the UAE one of the most innovative nations in the world.

The award is mainly assessing companies' innovation levels against the three major award criteria of Innovation Capabilities, Innovation Drivers, and Innovation Results, under the governance of judging committee members. Participating companies will be awarded from one to five stars based on scores achieved. The award framework and criteria have been developed to assess the overall innovation maturity level of private sector companies while the comprehensive feedback report will help companies to identify their innovation strengths and performance gaps. In addition, this, the annual Ideas Arabia Competition 2018, is conducted yearly along with the annual conference, to recognize the most significant ideas implemented by companies during the previous year. This competition seeks to identify employees and organizations for their outstanding ideas. This competition provides an opportunity for participating companies to benchmark against other leading organizations, and acts as a motivational tool for employees. Participation in this competition had many benefits. It provided additional recognition to the employees, and highlights how involving the employees can benefit the organization. It helped in imparting one's experience to other companies, and provided an opportunity for one's employees to learn from practices followed in other organizations.

The innovation award framework consists of three main criteria with a total of 1000 points attainable. The first criterion focuses on the Innovation Capability, covering sub-criteria such as Funding, Training, Technology and Innovation Center, with a weight of 20 percent of the total award points. The second criterion focuses on five key Innovation Drivers with a total weight of 40 percent. The remaining 400 points is reserved for the Innovation Results Criterion, which includes three sub-criteria: Customer Results, Business Growth Results, and Community and Sustainability Results.

The UAE Innovation Award objectives are:

- support UAE National Innovation Strategy;
- promote innovation culture throughout UAE private sector organizations;
- raise the level of innovation practices based on the award framework and standards;
- strengthen organizations' innovation capabilities to create sustainable value for their customers;
- recognize and reward the leading innovative companies in UAE;
- build and maintain a strong network of Innovation professionals and qualified assessors.

In the first cycle of award, following companies were awarded in the respective categories (Table 5.1).

Table 5.1 UAE innovation award winners, 2017

The 2 star companies	3 star winners	4 star winners	5 star winners
Dubai Silicon Oasis Authority British Orchard Nursery The ENTERTAINER	Aster Pharmacies Group LLC Emirates Central Cooling Systems Corporation Emirates NBD Mashreq Bank	Global Food Industries The Emirates Group Emirates Global Aluminum Dubai Cable Company (Private) Limited	Borouge Pvt. Ltd

Source: Dubai Quality Group

5.3 ASQ Innovation Award

ASQ UAE innovation award was launched to recognize team efforts in promoting innovation within their organizations and creating new value for their customers and business, by ASQ UAE Local Member Community and Mrs. Nancy Nouaimeh, Country Counselor of ASQ in UAE. In 2015, ASQ UAE Quality Professionals Award became the first award for ASQ in the region and outside the Americas. Following this, after a successful first two cycles expanding ASQ UAE Awards to include Team Innovation, ASQ UAE Innovation Award both for teams in private and public sectors entities was established by the ASQ Board of Directors approval, two years after the Country Leaders had established a clear agenda for Innovation for UAE.

The initial ASQ UAE Team Innovation Award inaugural cycle was launched in April 2017 and had a scope limited to organizations within UAE, from both private and public sectors. Award purpose as approved was "to recognize the achievements, efforts and contribution of Quality and other Professionals in UAE in the field of Innovation of products/services/processes". The Award was established in a partnership with Dubai Economy. In 2018, after the success of the first cycle launched in 2017 at the UAE level only, ASQ saw an opportunity in expanding the Award scope to include applicants from organizations operating in the entire Middle East and Africa region, sponsored by ASQ Middle East and Africa (MEA) office. Award framework eligibility was then modified accordingly, and the Award name became "ASQ MEA Innovation Award" with a model aiming to support Innovative teams and organizations showcase their organization-wide innovation maturity and the use of a structured methodology for the execution of innovative projects leading to improved profitability and competitiveness of their organization.

The Award assessment has at its core five principles that govern all activities taken within each cycle:

5.3.1 Objectivity

The award has a clearly defined process, criteria and governing rules, including an independent quality assurance mechanism to avoid subjectivity and the influence of personal opinions in the nominations evaluation process. Measures to ensure anonymity of nominations were taken into consideration while developing the award application.

5.3.2 Fairness

The award criteria and scoring process have been established with diligent efforts to ensure the nominations evaluation process is carried out in a just manner that reflects the credibility of the award.

5.3.3 Transparency

The award process offers utmost transparency in all its milestones, applicants will be made aware of their application status and the results of the evaluation process and scoring in a timely manner. Applicant questions, if any, will be addressed in an accurate and direct manner.

5.3.4 Independency

An independent Quality Award (QA) professional is assigned to audit the award process and ensure compliance with the award set principles.

5.3.5 High Standards and Performance

With its thorough criteria and objective scoring process, the award incorporates high performance standards that guarantee the award winners a distinguished recognition in quality.

To ensure a high level of objectivity and integrity, supporting documents as evidence are sought from the applicant team, and several levels of assessments ensure there is no conflict of interest. In addition, the shortlisted are requested to present their successful innovation projects in front of the Award jury.

The main goals and objectives of the award are:

- Provide recognition for teams/professionals in organizations with demonstrated good practices and systems that foster a culture that supports innovation and lead to creating new values for the organizations and its customers. And that by implementing innovative products/services and processes.
- Motivate quality and innovation professionals and organizations to implement innovation strategies, tools and methodologies in various industries.
- Drive improvement of innovation practices and systems in the organizations operating in the region and contribute positively to the National Innovation agendas.
- Moreover, ASQ will gain visibility in UAE and the Middle East and the African region and reinforce its reputation as the "Global Voice of Quality."

After all, quality professionals strive to make the world a better place for individuals and organizations. By promoting innovation too, the Society brings a clear message on the wide impact of system thinking and good management system on the sustainability of innovation efforts, marrying hence the concepts of quality, excellence, and innovation. And it became clear over the last decade that innovation can also help address major global challenges such as climate change, energy, security and health, by boosting income and productivity growth, which are key to a sustainable, happy and fulfilled society.

The main two benefits for applicants of this award are:

1. Assess and benchmark locally and regionally their innovation practices, management system, and team performance.
2. Gain regional recognition for their organization's innovation efforts.

The ASQ Award: A Profile of Nancy, a Passionate Leader of Quality and Practitioner at Abela & Co

Nancy Nouaimeh is a Chartered Business Excellence Professional with a focus on continuous improvement at both personal and professional levels. An AVP-Quality, Safety and Performance Excellence at a leading food services management company, Nancy holds Masters' degrees in Agronomic Sciences and Bioengineering and Total Quality Management.

Nancy is an accomplished quality, excellence, and business performance improvement professional and an experienced safety professional, with over fifteen years of experience; twelve in the food sector and five in scientific research in an academic environment. Nancy led improvement projects through innovative and integrated approaches to achieve service and business excellence and has expertise in strategy deployment, continuous improvement methodologies, CSR, Lean tools, ISO standards, and auditing and supplier management. She is a talented coach and trainer well versed in leading teams and transferring knowledge across the organization.

Nancy believes in continuous learning and has achieved many certifications across the years. She has a track record of volunteering activities in UAE both for quality through her ASQ member leader role, and for women empowerment as a member of UAE Women's Empowerment Principles Taskforce.

She has won several awards:

- American Society for Quality (ASQ)
  - Fresh Faces in Quality: one of the forty-six quality professionals nominated: Quality Progress (ASQ), Nov. 2016.
  - ASQ UAE-Local Member Community Chair (various roles since 2011).
- Main role is to provide leadership and support, to the Local Members Communities, and organize added-value activities such as knowledge-sharing seminars, Communities of Practices, and World Quality Day Celebrations.
  - ASQ MEA Awards (Team Innovation and Quality Professional): Co-established, developed and assessed award nominations, since 2015.
  - ASQ Regional Conference Technical Committee Member: served on the committee on ASQ MEA Regional Quality Conference, since 2015.
  - Testimonial Leadership Award: awarded from ASQ, for serving on ASQ Strategy Deployment Committee in 2015.
- Testimonial Leadership Award: awarded from ASQ, for leading the Local Members Community team and initiatives in Dubai in 2014, a role handled from 2011 to 2015.

5.3.6 Award Process and Overview of Criterion

The award has the following eligibility criteria for applicants:

- a team of professionals from any function, field, industry and experience;
- a team project for implementation of process and product/service innovation;
- can be employed in a small- to medium- or large-size organization;
- organizations from private or public sector;
- organizations from the Middle East and Africa regions.

Further, the award framework was designed based on a set of criteria that covers the elements of a proper management system, an innovation-driven team project, and results achieved for both. These were grouped in two distinct areas as per the illustration below:

5.3.7 Enablers (Five Criteria)

The applicant is required to describe all the enablers that are deployed to ensure an efficient innovation process is being established by the organization to achieve the vision, strategy, and objectives set for innovation and to achieve a high level of innovation system maturity. The main questions to be answered are:

E1: How does the leadership of the organization support the innovation process within the organization?
E2: How does the organization manage strategically its innovation program? And how does it establish accountabilities for innovation?
E3: What investment is made by the organization of the applicant to enable innovation?
E4: What Innovation Management System is in place? What is its implementation process and extent of deployment?
E5: How does the organization build competencies in innovation?

E6: How does the organization manage its collaboration/partnerships with external stakeholders to advance innovation?
E7: How does the organization learn from past experiences in innovation and share knowledge internally?

5.3.8 Results/Impact (Three Criteria)

R1: Segmented results for innovation projects completed by the applying team and for the entire organization.
R2: Number of products/services and/or processes innovated per year; provided for the past three years for the entire organization.
R3: Sales, revenues, and savings generated as result of innovation efforts and projects, and demonstrate sustainability of results.

The Assessment process: The Award assessment is carried out following a three-steps process:

- Initial screening by Award's Manager to ensure guidelines have been met.
- Detailed evaluation and scoring done by independent team constituted of two competent assessors.
- Shortlisted applicants are requested to defend their applications in front of the esteemed jury constituted of international experts.

A minimum qualifying score is specified for every cycle, and each applicant should reach this score in order to be eligible. No recognition will be granted if no one achieves the minimum qualifying score.

A maximum of three awards are planned to be given out each year in each of the sub-categories:

- UAE and MEA (other countries than UAE)
- Private- and public-sector organizations

The winners of the ASQ award are:

Dubai Silicone Oasis Authority (DSOA): Dubai Silicon Oasis Authority (DSOA), a 100 percent government-owned free zone, was established following Law no. 16 of 2005 of the Government of Dubai, with the Mission to "facilitate and promote modern technology-based industries" thus supporting the region's demand for business expansion. A full package of incentives and benefits are provided to companies operating within the free zone. Dubai Silicon Oasis (DSO) is a technology park and provides both a living and working integrated community.

Dubai Silicon Oasis is designed as a hi-tech ecosystem which offers businesses a plethora of advantages including a state-of-the-art infrastructure, in-house business services, and strong business support such as technology investment incentives for large enterprises, entrepreneurial support, an incubation center, and venture capital funding.

Role of applying team:

The Innovation Department was established to create, capture, and cultivate innovation culture within DSOA by addressing organizational growth gap through business-driven innovation. The team collaborated with the idea of generators/implementers of innovative projects used as a core for the application for ASQ UAE Team Innovation Award in 2017.

Innovation Management History at DSOA:

- In 2012, Dubai Silicon Oasis Authority (DSOA) leadership took a significant leap forward by establishing an innovation section within the organization, led by an innovation specialist. DSOA was the first free zone in the UAE with such a visionary initiative.
- In 2013, innovation was officially added as one of the DSOA corporate values—a strategic decision to show the DSOA employees that innovation should be embedded into their daily activities and culture within the organization.

- This was backed with the appointment of an innovation champion in each department whose main role is to be the innovation ambassador within their departments. Currently, DSOA have twenty innovation champions in the organization.
- A new DSOA Innovation Strategy was developed in 2015 and endorsed by DSOA management. An alignment with the UAE National Strategy, Dubai 2021 Vision, and DSOA Corporate Strategy was made to support national innovation vision and programs as well as help close the growth gap in DSOA through value-creation innovation.

The innovation strategy is translated into tactical plans through various programs and initiatives. Furthermore, objectives and KPIs are defined, monitored, measured, and communicated regularly to the management through our One-Page Plan (OPP). With the management's guidance and approval, the budget is allocated annually and sufficiently to endorse programs that cultivate innovation cultures and support idea creation and implementation that would benefit the organization. DSOA's six building blocks of the innovation model work as pillars to propel innovation, cultivate innovation culture, and create values from it. The six building blocks consist of business sponsors, tools and processes, human capital, communication, recognition, and measurement. The DSOA leadership have demonstrated their commitment in promoting innovation culture in every block.

Innovation at Kimoha: Kimoha Entrepreneurs Ltd., Dubai (KEL). This is an ISO 9001:2008 certified company. It is a pioneer in manufacturing and marketing plain and printed self-adhesive labels and flexibles for packaging applications, plus paper products for retail and office use. It is complemented by providing Auto ID equipment and solutions for virtually all industries and commercial establishments, and more importantly, products for the aviation industries such as baggage tags, boarding passes, etc. Kimoha leadership encourages all its employees to be change agents and firmly believes that solutions can be provided efficiently and effectively with commitment and leadership. Many approaches are in place by KEL leadership to promote a culture of innovation:

- Creating a climate for change: Kimoha has an open-door policy for all its employees. It branded its innovation program as *Aavishkar* (an Indian word which means innovation). Anyone can suggest a novel idea, or give recommendations to improve/challenge current practices. A *think tank* room and an *aavishkar* room were set up to generate ideas, develop solutions, and to set up a library (in line with the "Reading" strategy of UAE Rulers).
- Innovation at Kimoha is intended to (i) solve a pressing problem for the customer, (ii) add value to customers by understanding their needs. This is done through the following different activities promoting a culture of excellence:
  - Engage early with customers and be a part of the process.
  - Invest in developing innovative samples, artworks for the customer, and demonstrate the new value, till they are satisfied to place orders.
  - Invest in technology and build capability for Research & Development.
  - Use latest eco-friendly technologies, where feasible.
  - Absorb development cost, and not to look at immediate profits, but rather seek long-term profitability.
  - Develop a business/operating model such that innovative products and services are sustainable and generate revenue/profits,
  - Engage with other stakeholders where needed.
  - Encourage cross-functional collaboration.

5.4 Leading for Innovation: What It Is, What It Is Not—a Case of Dubai Quality Group

Innovation awards are indeed crucial to promote innovation culture. Hence it is imperative to understand from leaders of innovation: What roles are to be played to promote innovation? Why is it so important to celebrate innovation and the companies that are exercising it? How do they think they would help to shape businesses' attitudes towards innovation? How are the companies looking to establish best working practices, as well as foster a culture of creativity in the workplace? In this section we will get to understand this from Fatma Buti Al Mheiri—Chairman of Dubai Quality Group.

Fatma Al Mheiri's ambition is to be an inspiration for success and excellence and achievement is her driving force in life. During her professional journey spanning eighteen years, she excelled in her studies due to her love for learning, and holds several business degrees.

She gained a wealth of experience in the local and federal government sector as well as in in the private sector in the fields of strategic planning and business excellence. Her continuous achievements in her career, holding various senior positions, resulted in her being elected as the first young woman Emirati Chairman of Dubai Quality Group, in addition to her current roles as the director, Investment & CSR Department, in the Social Benefit & Empowerment Sector, and 10X Team Leader at the Community Development Authority, Dubai. She brings to the table extensive experience working with all organizational levels, creating, promoting, and delivering solutions designed to support the organization's business plan.

As 10X Team Leader, her goal is to meet the needs of the future, and her ten-year plan will see to the development of work systems to meet those needs in a manner that ensures the continuity of the life of prosperity enjoyed by residents of the UAE.

"We have achieved a quantum leap in terms of empowering individuals and activating the frameworks that enable Dubai to transfer its pioneering experience to the world regarding the empowerment of people", Fatma commented.

"The outputs of 10X will not only benefit the population of Dubai but also the world by creating data-driven platforms regarding human development to bring out the best in the people," she added.

Fatma has formed and facilitated twenty-two Excellence and Performance teams at the Dubai international airport, and she has led the initiative of improving Dubai airport's position from twenty-three to number one amongst fifty-two international airports from the same size and number of annual passengers. As the Chairman of Dubai Quality Group (DQG), she is planning to maintain and strengthen the position of DQG as the primary Excellence and Quality player in the region, by expanding its services to include event management and consulting.

In 1997, Fatma graduated from the Higher Colleges of Technology, Dubai Women's College, with a Higher Diploma in Business Administration and received her Bachelor of Applied Science in Business Administration degree in 1999 from the same College. She was awarded her Master in International Business from the University of Wollongong in Dubai, in 2003.

Her passion to create an interactive and enjoyable business environment that supports progress is key to her success, and her managerial strengths, growing from one success to the next over the previous eighteen years, has enhanced her leadership skills and led her to be an exceptional leader during her professional journey.

DQG successfully organized an "award awareness" session for more than eighty-three companies that showed a keen interest to participate, discussing the extensive award framework, criteria, and guidelines for submission. The attendance to these sessions has been overwhelming considering that this is the first year of the award and is a clear indicator of the importance innovation has gained in the private sector recently. Additionally, DQG organized three intensive workshops, training more than 118 assessors from sixteen different nationalities for the award. The Chairman strongly believes that innovation is the only way to build a great history in the UAE, and that innovation has become a crucial measure of the performance of an economy, and one of the decisive factors in the development process. According to

Fatma's celebration of innovations and innovators in the UAE promotes the nation's creative thinkers, encourages an innovation culture as a defining element in the UAE society, whilst also recognizing the organizations that are executing it by helping these companies to identify their innovation strengths and performance gaps, in order to enforce Dubai's transformation into the world capital of innovation.

Under the 2018 slogan "Innovation Starts with You," the UAE Innovation Month is the largest celebration of its kind that seeks to celebrate the best ideas on innovation from the government and private sectors as well as from the public, and is organized under the directives of His Highness Shaikh Mohammad Bin Rashid Al Maktoum, Vice-President and Prime Minister of the UAE and Ruler of Dubai. The Chairman explains that the nationwide celebration of innovation focuses primarily on the seven major sectors of the National Innovation Strategy: health, transportation, renewable energy, technology, education, water, and space. DQG celebrates the innovation by organizing the "UAE Innovation Award" complementing the initiatives launched by the UAE Government to provide an institutional infrastructure for innovation.

The UAE is determined to be one of the most innovative countries, to emerge as a global innovation hub, and have all the elements to speed up the transformation, especially in light of the "National Innovation Strategy" that was launched by the UAE government in October 2014. The UAE were ranked first in the region as per the 2017 Global Innovation Index, and has worked tirelessly to spread the culture of excellence, creativity, and innovation.

Fatma's vision for the Innovation Awards is that it will enforce the public and private sectors in the UAE to be at the forefront of international organizations in innovation and that it is possible due to the UAE's history, cutting-edge knowledge, and expertise in various innovation-driven industries.

According to her, the goal of the innovation award is threefold: To promote innovation and expand its applications across fifteen sectors in the private sector; to encourage and embrace initiatives and innovative projects; and lastly, to enable the UAE to be a model for creative thinking and innovation on both the regional and global levels.

Sharing her thoughts, Fatma said that the legacy of the innovation awards is in innovation as it facilitates a qualitative shift in the methods of production, increases productivity, and thus enhances the national product competitiveness in global markets. Innovation leads to the development of the individuals' quality of life and increases the economic welfare rates.

The concept of smart, imaginative thinking to devise inventions or solutions, is considered critical to helping the UAE diversify its economy and further cement its position as a global powerhouse. While the UAE's foot is firmly on the innovation accelerator, there are some glaring sectors that require far more nurturing by shaping business attitudes into innovation which is an effective strategy to compete.

Fatma explained that shaping the businesses' attitudes towards innovation management is necessary for firms to efficiently respond to external or internal opportunities, and use their creative efforts to introduce new products, services, or processes. According to her:

- Firms need to be able to scan and search their internal and external environments to detect signals about potential innovation.
- Firms need to select from this set of potential innovation projects those which will be carried out further.
- Firms need to provide the resources to exploit the project, either through internal R&D or by acquiring the necessary technology.
- Firms have to implement the innovation throughout the various stages of development to final launch, and to ensure that the organization is able to capture the returns emerging from that innovation.

It is now widely accepted that innovation is an interactive process, involving constant feedback loops between the different phases. Moreover, innovation management is not only about Research and Development (R&D), as it involves employees at every level in contributing creatively to a company's development, manufacturing, and marketing, as well as constant interaction with the market and other external key players.

Based on Fatma's own experience, the most appropriate innovation management approach will depend on the firm's size, the sector of activity, culture, as well as the type of innovation that the firm wants to focus on. Innovation is a broad concept that can take many forms, ranging from product to process innovation, as well as innovation in marketing and organization and can also be classified as attending to the novelty of the knowledge involved, and this in turn, influences the scope of innovation management.

Fatma highlighted that innovation is the main key to a prosperous and profitable organization and that it is essential to carry out and adopt new methods to ensure progress. She is very optimistic about DQG's ability to lead the change in order to promote a culture of innovation.

Dubai Quality Group (DQG) was established as a non-profit organization by Dubai Economy in 1994, under the patronage of H.H. Sheikh Ahmed Bin Saeed Al Maktoum, President of Dubai Civil Aviation Authority, Chairman of Dubai Airports, Chairman and Chief Executive of Emirates Airline & Group with the aim to develop and promote quality and business excellences practices in UAE.

She believes DQG has a lot of potential and since its establishment, it has expanded its global reach by aligning its Vision, Mission & Strategy with the UAE's Vision 2021 "Innovate to lead". Accordingly, the group has set higher goals for the future, targeting the integration of innovation within the group in order to maximize members' satisfaction. DQG's mission is to empower, sustain world-class practices in business excellence, and provide knowledge-sharing platforms.

Innovation is considered to be a major cornerstone in all their awards including:

- Ideas Arabia 12th International Conference & Competition 2017: eleven winners were awarded by Sheikh Saeed bin Hasher bin Maktoum Al Maktoum.
- UAE Ideas Conference & Award 2017: H.H. Sheikh Eng. Salem Bin Sultan Al Qasimi inaugurated the 6th cycle of this award and honoured ten government entities. The conference showcases how Emirati innovation is the cornerstone for the nation's sustainability.
- Ninth Global Continual Improvement & Innovation Symposium 2017: fourteen entities won out of one hundred participants and gained hands-on experience in global business innovation in various categories including: Kaizen, Innovation, Lean Six Sigma, Best Practice Management, and Happiness.
- Under the theme "Making Change Happen: Implementing Change Management", the Change Management Subgroup organized the 6th Change Management Conference 2017.
- Fourteenth Emirates Women Awards 2017: honouring nine extraordinary women professionals and entrepreneurs from 110 participants. The award aims to highlight women in leadership roles and to recognize leading Emirati and expat women for their outstanding contribution to the UAE.

The Chairman highlighted the award is in harmony with other national initiatives within the framework of UAE Vision 2021 and national innovation strategy, aiming at promoting innovation and driving sustainable development in UAE, along with improving the competitiveness of the private sector organizations. The innovation award framework and criteria are designed based on world-class innovation concepts and best practices which will bring great benefits to participating companies, their customers, staff, and UAE community.

Innovation has become a trend across the world, including in the UAE, which launched the Year of Innovation in 2015 with the goal of making UAE one of the most innovative nations in the world by 2021. The UAE Innovation Month seeks to foster innovation with more than 1000 activities across the nation. It's an innovation festival, involving government entities, the private sector, small businesses, multinationals, business bodies, and individuals intended to promote the UAE as a hub for creative thinking.

The benefits of celebrating innovation month include:

- profit/margins increase;
- product diversification;
- product differentiation;
- satisfying consumer needs;
- keeping or increasing market quota;
- securing a market strategic position;
- use of new business opportunities;
- markets development;
- personalized services;
- increase of competitive advantage;
- use of economies of scale.

DQG's aim is to sustain world-class business excellence practices through partnerships, networking, and knowledge sharing, and Fatma's view is that partnership with the DQG is a clear demonstration of an organization's commitment to quality improvement and business excellence.

Since its inception in 1994, DQG has been spreading the culture of quality and giving awards of excellence to myriad public and private sector institutions in Dubai and globally by bringing the latest knowledge from all over the world through strategic partnerships with international entities such as the European Foundation for Quality Management (EFQM), American Society of Quality (ASQ), Global Benchmarking Network (GBN), Institute of Directors (India), Ideas UK, Ideas America, Business Process Improvement Resource, etc.

In association with the United Nations Development Programme in Iraq, the Dubai Quality Group customized the EFQM Excellence

Training programme for sixteen delegates from Iraq's General Secretariat of Ministers Council. Through this customized programme,sixteen Iraqi delegates qualified as internationally accredited assessors. Another initiative from DQG was organizing a Benchmarking Program in association with DEWA and KHDA to share their best practices and journey towards excellence with Iraqi's delegates.

Under Fatma's leadership, DQG signed several partnerships with government entities in line with the "Year of Giving." Dubai Economy and Dubai Quality Group signed an agreement to strengthen their participation in community welfare activities with the aim to implement the directives of the President of the UAE, His Highness Sheikh Khalifa bin Zayed Al Nahyan.

Dubai South also signed a memorandum of understanding (MOU) with Dubai Quality Group with both parties exchanging expertise to work towards adopting quality standards and excellence. The Dubai Government Excellence Program also signed an MOU with Dubai Quality Group during the Dubai Forum for Government Best Practices.

Fatma commented that they were ready to cooperate with all bodies including non-members, to be part of the business growth and excellence in the region, and to engage people and boost knowledge exchange. She said that there is a vast community out there who can take advantage of their organization since they implement systematic suggestion schemes in institutions where employees are rewarded for innovation, as well as continual improvement symposiums.

DQG has close links with professional bodies and academic institutes, both locally and internationally and it provides an excellent environment for its partners to meet and exchange ideas, information, and expertise. It is a forum where all types of organizations can benefit from each other.

DQG's approach is to partner with all types of organizations that are making a difference and support their initiatives in terms of promoting local culture, quality, business excellence, and innovation.

Fatma believes that partnerships, networking, and knowledge sharing is the best way for the UAE's business community to thrive. The UAE has one of the largest, most open, and fastest growing economies in the Middle East and North Africa (MENA) region. The UAE is the largest logistics hub in the MENA region, and the country's location is accessible for major regional markets.

In Fatma's opinion, the best working practice means finding and using the best ways of working to achieve your business objectives. It involves keeping up to date with the ways that successful businesses operate, in your own sector as well as others, and measuring your ways of working against those used by the market leaders.

Her advice to companies who are keen to establish best practices, is to apply it through technical standards, management standards, and benchmarking.

She said that applying best practice means learning from and through the experience of others, and that one way of doing this is through benchmarking, which allows you to compare your business with other successful businesses to highlight areas where your business could improve.

Applying the appropriate standards to your business will enable you to apply best practice across the organization, and to work against objective criteria to achieve manufacturing or service quality.

Applying the best practice strategy, she said, can help the organizations to become more competitive, increase its sales and develop new markets, reduce costs and become more efficient, improve the skills of its workforce, use technology more effectively, reduce waste and improve quality, and respond more quickly to innovations.

There are several business tools that companies can use to achieve management best practice, including: benchmarking, forecasting, financial planning, strategic planning, and performance monitoring.

In her opinion, a good approach to creating a value-driven workplace and making any organization more "value-focused", is by fostering a culture of creativity which is the only path to creating a workplace culture that encourages the kind of personal and strategic risk-taking that creativity requires.

She also advises that firms should do their best to create a culture where creativity is encouraged so that employees feel that their ideas are valued, their minds are engaged, and their thoughts are respected.

Employees who work in creative environments are more likely to come up with innovative ideas. They also develop the flexibility to adapt to changes in the marketplace; that same flexibility can make your business more agile and better able to compete in a constantly changing business world.

Being the first female chair of DQG and a 10X Team Leader, Fatma said that this is the perfect time for young Emirati women to be inspired by achievements of women Emirati leaders and to show what they can do for their country.

Today, UAE women are seizing the opportunity to prove to the world what they're made of as the UAE provides a safe and nurturing environment for women to empower, innovate, and excel. According to her, Emirati women leaders have done the UAE proud by being champions of progress and innovation. She said that since 2015, the UAE proudly ranks number one in the region for women in leading roles according to a study that was conducted in 132 countries across the world, and based on recent statistics from the World Economic Forum, the UAE tops the list for treating women with respect while the world debates about gender equality.

Fatma's story and achievements as a female leader is inspiring and serves as encouragement for young females to follow in her successful footsteps as ambassadors for empowerment, innovation, and excellence.

5.5 Innovation Profile of Ducab

Jointly owned by the Investment Corporation of Dubai and Senaat (General Holding Corporation, Abu Dhabi), Ducab is a global leader in the development, design, manufacture, marketing, and distribution of copper and aluminium wire and cable products. Ducab operates six manufacturing facilities across four sites in the UAE with all its production based within the country. Employing over 1500 people, the company serves customers worldwide in the fields of energy, general construction, oil and gas, renewables, industrial, defence, rail transport, marine, mining, and other specialty industry verticals.

As of 2018, Ducab Group comprises of several business units: Ducab Wires and Cables; Ducab High Voltage (HV), a joint venture between Ducab, Dubai Electricity and Water Authority (DEWA), and Abu Dhabi Water and Electricity Authority (ADWEA); Ducab Metals, which supplies copper rod and wire to the region; and Ducab Aluminium Company (DAC), a joint venture between Ducab and Senaat which manufactures aluminium rods and conductors.

Ducab has a manufacturing capability of over 115,000 metal tonnes of high, medium, and low voltage cables and 110,000 tonnes of copper rod and wire per annum, promoting specialized cables such as PetroBICC (oil, gas, and petrochemical sector), RuBICC (flexible rubber cables), FlamBICC (fire performance cables), MarineBICC (for marine and shipbuilding) and NuBICC (sixty-year certified cable range for nuclear power plants).

Ducab is an ISO 9001 certified company and is also certified to the ISO 14001 Environmental Management System and the OHSAS 18001 Occupational Health and Safety. Ducab cables are also approved by international third-party certification bodies such as: LPCB, BASEC, and Lloyd's Register (UK), DNV and KEMA (Netherlands), and ABS, UL (USA).

Ducab participated in the first UAE Innovation Award competition in 2017, and won a Four-Star Award.

DUCAB Innovation Strategy

Ducab's 2018–2022 strategy, and specifically the company's innovation strategy, is the foundation for all the company's efforts around fostering innovation. These efforts are based around four priorities:

1. Customer centricity: To meet customers' need in various markets.
2. Industry: To respond to market dynamics and cable industry challenges.
3. Technology: To adopt breakthrough technologies.
4. Sustainability: To drive company growth through social and environmental responsibility.

Innovation in Ducab is based on the fully established and well-known "Ten Types of Innovation" framework:

1. Services	6. Product system
2. Product performance	7. Processes
3. Structure	8. Network
4. Profit model	9. Brand
5. Channel	10. Customer engagement

To cover the ten individual or potential combinations of innovation types, a multidisciplinary structure, including both external and internal stakeholders, was developed:

The innovation committee fosters innovation culture across the business aspiring to:

- get a deeper understanding of the customers and to provide solutions tailored to their needs;
- observe early movers;
- engage with young start-up companies;
- create stretch goals which can challenge our employees;
- foster creativity without losing control;
- have well-defined sandboxes for experimentation.

The main role of the committee is to review and filter various proposals and assign specified tasks to the dedicated cross-functional teams and working groups for assessment, development, and implementation.

Another important role is also to look for feedback and to transfer the stakeholders' view to the process owners for further improvement.

As the first step, all ideas and suggestions for innovative work are discussed at an innovation forum. Representatives of all departments and process owners in Ducab are members of the forum.

Ducab's cross-functional innovation teams include PhD, MSc, and BSc holders with more than one hundred years of cumulative experience in research and development. They are supported by engineers with electrical, mechanical, and polymer backgrounds, experts in finance, marketing, supply, sales, and the human resource area. Specific teams are linked internally and externally, which gives various opportunities and benefits:

- Direct technical collaboration with customers for product and service innovation.
- Internal process improvement projects that allows employees to connect to each other, express their ideas, and try out concepts.
- Access to technology such as manufacturing equipment, test laboratories, external type-test laboratories, and technical libraries.
- Access to machine manufacturers and material suppliers to support the innovation process.

- Networking opportunities in exhibitions and conferences.
- Collaboration with universities in UAE and abroad.

DUCAB in the Innovation Area

INNOVATION CAPABILITIES

The annual budget at Ducab supports a wide range of expenditures associated with innovation programs. This includes capital expenditure on plant and test facilities to ensure that products supplied by Ducab are compliant with global best practices. Funds are also invested in research and development activities under the heading of the Product and Technology Development Department with eight dedicated employees. To support this innovation work, there is a team of sixteen manufacturing engineers, seven test engineers, fifty quality technicians, and three quality system engineers. They spend approximately 50 percent of their time on routine production and 50 percent on development work.

Ducab's annual budget also covers activities in problem-solving techniques as well as leadership training. Other activities designed to encourage an atmosphere of innovative thinking include off-site team-building sessions.

Some examples of trainings in specific areas:

- lean manufacturing;
- six sigma
- quality tool training such as cause and effect analysis, statistical process control;
- constraint management;
- off-site initiative and teambuilding courses;
- operational excellence;
- quality control and assurance (by national and international certification and accreditation bodies).

In addition to the above planned budget allocations, Ducab management reserves provisions for innovation projects which are of strategic importance as approved by the board of directors.

Product innovation in Ducab is applied in three ways:

- Optimization to existing product and production processes to increase yield and improve cost effectiveness. These are short-term projects which do not seek to alter the standard against which the product is made.
- Enhancement of existing products to a higher performing standard, or to satisfy new market requirements. These are medium-term projects which may require some capital investment.
- Development of new products to gain access to new market areas. These are long-term projects which may require investment in a whole new production facility.

Ducab is partnering with various customers and stakeholders in expansion of its manufacturing capabilities and also product range. Examples include:

- Ducab High Voltage (DHV) manufacturing of high and extra high voltage cables, partnering between Dubai Electricity and Water Authority (DEWA): 25 percent and Abu Dhabi Water and Electricity Authority (ADWEA): 25 percent and Ducab: 50 percent.
- Ducab Aluminium Company (DAC): production of aluminium and aluminium alloy rods, wires and conductors: partnership between Senaat: 40 percent and Ducab:60 percent.

Ducab has a robust new product development procedure to ensure a systematic approach to launching new products. The procedure uses the input of expert knowledge from a range of functions within the company to establish the viability of a project prior to actively commencing with development work.

Ducab has invested in building state of the art facilities to support product development work:

- nine specialized test labs across Ducab Group, including a fire test lab;
- advanced materials analysing testing equipment;
- lab-scale extruders;

- manufacturing plant and equipment for large-scale trials;
- brainstorming/debate rooms;
- a technical library;
- upstream facilities such as a copper rod plant, PVC compound facility, and an aluminium rod plant.

INNOVATION DRIVERS

In line with the UAE national agenda, Ducab is committed to being one of the key players in promoting innovation, research and development, and strengthening the regulatory framework for the cables industry.

The executive management team at Ducab is committed to leading and promoting the company's innovation strategy to support sustainable growth. The same has been reflected in Ducab's mission statement, quality policy, and values.

Ducab leaders are a role model to innovation amongst employees, as seen in their participation in the innovation meetings and strategies development process. This has included the support of Ducab leaders in developing the sixty-years life performance nuclear cable products, which has positively impacted a unique project recognized locally from the Emirates Nuclear Energy Corporation (ENEC) and globally by KHNP (Korean Hydro Nuclear Power), and KEPCO (Korean Electric Power Corporation) utilities.

As a result, Ducab's product portfolio maintains a significant number of projects, developed based on the needs of the UAE national agenda to preserve the environment and safety of citizens. These specialized product portfolios include:

- NuBICC & SolarBICC for clean energy;
- FlamBICC and fire-resistant cables;
- RuBICC for railways, ports, and infrastructure;
- PetroBICC to protect the environment and reduce hazardous material in the oil, gas, and petrochemical industries.

Ducab has always partnered with the community in various ways. Participating in exhibitions is used as a platform for showcasing products, services, and gaining new knowledge to enhance innovative ideas and new opportunities across the globe. Below are some of the exhibitions that Ducab participates in:

1. Middle East Electricity Exhibition (MEEE): a gold sponsor.
2. Water Energy Technology and Environment Exhibition (WETEX): a strategic sponsor for the last four years
3. Abu Dhabi International Petroleum Exhibition and Conference (ADIPEC).
4. Cable and Wire Fair-India.

INNOVATION RESULTS

Delivering value to Ducab's customers is the most important task in the company's innovation work. Some of Ducab's recent success stories include:

- Ducab is the preferred supplier by many clients, and our customer satisfaction surveys are a testament to this. Because of exceptional performance, Ducab gets repeat business from many of its clients.
- Ducab takes pride in being the first cable company in the Middle East to develop and supply nuclear cables to Barakah nuclear power plant. The cables were developed successfully with approvals from Kinetrics Lab, Canada. The cables met sixty+ years life-cycle testing, requiring extensive documentation submission and safe records storage, which was handled in a robust manner.
- Korea Electric Power Corporation (KEPCO) has awarded Ducab with repeat orders for nuclear power plants in Korea.
- Ducab supplies fire resistant cables under the brand name of FlamBICC. This innovative product is used in special applications where circuit integrity is required in the event of fire.

Ducab innovations are always linked with customers' engagement and close relationships:

- Ducab's export business has witnessed double-digit growth since 2016 including 11 percent growth in 2017.

- Ducab has supplied its product and services to twenty-eight different countries as of 2017, covering six continents.
- Ducab has been successful in making inroads in various new market segments. In order to cater to new clients in different geographical areas, innovative methods are used for ensuring client satisfaction.

  – Ducab designed and supplied medium voltage (MV) cables for the Australian market for use in a solar plant.
  – Special fire-resistant cables for the Australian market are developed under the brand name of FlamBICC-ANZ.
  – To qualify in the Algerian market, an innovative method of cable sample supply and actual usage in grid was conducted for a period of six months.

Ducab is also focused on supporting the industry in which it operates:

- Ducab cable brands are well known in the marketplace. The fire-resistant cables are branded as **FlamBICC** which goes hand in hand with fire safety awareness.
- Ducab has taken extra steps to work with civil defence departments by organizing "Power over Fire" campaigns with information videos and kiosks in a large truck.
- Various other well-known brands from Ducab are **Powerplus** for medium voltage cables, **Smokemaster** for special low smoke zero halogen cables, **DuPan** for panel wires, **MarineBICC** for marine cables, **PetroBICC** for oil, gas, and petrochemicals cables, **NuBICC** for nuclear cables, **RuBICC** for rubber cables, **DuFlex** for flexible cords.
- With the best reputation in the market for its product and services, Ducab has been voted as a UAE Superbrand consecutively seven times from over 1500 brands in the UAE. Ducab competed with big international names in an online poll and was awarded the Superbrand title for market presence, product quality, consumer confidence, accounting practices, customer loyalty, and market acceptance.

5.6 Conclusion

Innovation awards no doubt aim to foster an innovation culture within the society. Organizations can get inspired through these awards. While they provide a platform for recognition, it is imperative to know that adapting an award-based framework can help an organization to kick-start an innovation drive. Adapting to such frameworks can provide a systematic innovation deployment. However, though an award process and writing up an application can be cumbersome, it does drive an organization to assess and improve their various approaches. It gives firsthand information on how and what the organization is currently doing as well how it can plan its future path to achieve superior performance. Such award type assessment has several benefits. They provide an objective feedback report with an independent viewpoint. The awards assessment provides a "third person" or an independent view of an organization; hence it is the most powerful tool that an organization can use to understand its performance level. The award type of assessment also has other several benefits such that it provides a list of strengths and areas for improvement. Moreover, it is based on the collection of evidence and is therefore fairly robust. In addition, it provides an excellent communication document for internal and external use. Further, as we note from the participants of the UAE innovation award, each of them have key practices being pursued in relation to each of the criterions. They are evidenced and deep rooted in the organizations' culture.

Moreover, in UAE, innovation awards are encouraging and promoting a strong culture for innovativeness. The leaders are strongly supporting organizational growth based on the innovation portfolios of the company. Moving forward, this emphasis will continue to stir organizational as well as national level competiveness. Having a dynamic set of criterions to assess the future innovation profiles will be an added advantage.

References

Dubai Quality Group. 2018. www.dqg.ae

https://www.innovation.ca/about/news/governor-generals-innovation-awards-2018-recipients-announced

6

Sustaining Innovation and Future Research Implications

6.1 Introduction

Innovations have had a profound positive impact in enhancing services and products as well in improving the design processes for improved outputs. Today, the ability to innovate is one of the most important factors for creating competitive advantages and for the success of any enterprise. Innovation is necessary for the survival, growth, and development of companies and for enhancing the competitive position of the company (Petkovska 2015). Truly, a capability to continuously introduce innovation can help an organization gain competitive advantage in a changing environment. Moreover, innovation acts a catalyst for the advancement of all sectors—be they business, government or social encompassing industries, societies, and countries. That said, the success of innovation is concerned with how organizations can shape or influence the levers or enablers of innovation to become a sustainable innovative organization.

Given that corporate mantras such as "Innovate or Evaporate" are truly becoming reality, sustaining innovation is crucial and hence we will first explore and understand the challenges posed with sustaining innovation. Innovative capacity varies from company to company and it is determined

F. Lasrado, *Fostering Creativity and Innovation*,
https://doi.org/10.1007/978-3-319-99121-4_6

by a larger number of factors that can promote or constrain the innovation process in the enterprise (Petkovska, 2015). Most innovations fail and enterprises that don't innovate die (Estelyiová and Žižlavský 2012). So our next question in line is to explore what are the critical challenges for sustaining innovation? Which domain do they arise from? How do we cater to them? What do most innovative companies do? What lessons can we learn from them?

6.2 Lessons from Top Innovative Companies

High performing organizations thrive on innovation and innovation is at the heart of their success. Forbes, Boston Consulting Group, and KPMG research lists the world most innovative companies every year. What is that so different in these companies from others? How do they spark innovation? These companies indeed have measurable success beyond financial benefits since economic success is not the only good indicator for assessing innovation performance. So let us get the insights from the most innovation companies. Forbes identifies Tesla, Amazon, ServicecNow, Hindustan live, and Netflix among the top ten innovative companies of 2018. Similarly, the Boston Consulting Group (BCG) produces a survey listing the top fifty innovative companies. Some of the companies consistently featuring are Apple, Google, 3M, and Johnson & Johnson. They have all successfully developed cultures which have shaped them to be the most innovative organizations. There are several good practices which can provide starting points for many aspiring organizations to draw a path for innovation deployment. In this section therefore we will discuss a few key points that could help managers to strengthen their innovation deployment.

A consistently listed and a regular member of the BCG most innovative companies list is Johnson & Johnson, which was placed No. 29 in 2016. BCG (2018) reports that one of J&J's strongest long-time innovators and executive vice president and chief scientific officer, Paul Stoffels, attributes these success to several key points. Their focus is on high-impact medical breakthroughs emphasizing on bringing forward the proper technologies. The internal and external exchanges are strong at

J&J and they treat both these engagements as equally important, as they actively encourage their scientists to connect with the outside world. Moreover, management makes sure that innovation programs are strategically aligned with the company's business objectives.

There are others who have actively pursued digital and data revolutions to the transformation of their own industries such as BASF. Organizations can thus learn from these to transform their innovation performance. According to a BCG Report (2016), PepsiCo—another company regularly recognized among the top innovative companies in the world—has a spectacular five-year growth rate of 10.7 %, compared with the industry average of 2.3%. PepsiCo's strengths lies in the digitizations it applies to every part of the business. In PepsiCo's products and services, it wraps digital services around its products, relying on efficient core processes and similarly in its customer experience and strategy. As such, digital innovation is practiced in every part of the business, and it is impacting the bottom line.

One large global company that maintains a culture committed to innovation is the global consumer-products marketer Reckitt Benckiser. Its culture is built on four pillars:

1. Ideas can come from anywhere. The company believes innovation starts and ends with the consumer. Every employee is encouraged to be on the lookout for new ideas related not only to new products but also to ingredients and combinations, marketing concepts, and packaging. For example, the company is happy to take ideas from employees at any level, plus from customers, suppliers, and academic experts. It maintains "idealink," an open, web-based platform in seven languages where anyone can submit innovation ideas.
2. Speed is paramount. Fast decision-making processes are based on an organizational structure that gives substantial independence to regional and national teams. Moreover, the regional structure enables speed by grouping together markets with similar characteristics, such as the developed markets of North America and Europe. This structure, for example, enabled the company to acquire US-based supplements company Schiff in December 2013, integrate it by May 2013, and by November announce that the company's successful

heart-health supplement, MegaRed, would be introduced in more than twenty markets across Europe by early 2014.
3. The company competes both defensively and offensively in each of its markets and categories, using innovation to spearhead its offense. It seeks to intimately understand competitors and their strategies; it backs its products, including new products, with aggressive marketing trade budgets; and it rewards aggressive execution through a variable-compensation scheme that includes incentives up to three times higher than what its major competitors offer.
4. It puts a high value on lean operations, maintaining an entrepreneurial spirit that emphasizes cost control.

On a similar line, Shell has established an "idea portal" called GameChanger through which employees can submit ideas through a website to a group of twenty-five full-time professionals in each of Shell's primary business sectors. It has an annual budget of $40 million. Employees are permitted to take time away from their day jobs to explore ideas. As proposals turn into business plans, employees may receive $300,000 to $500,000 in initial funding from GameChanger. Some 10 percent of ventures leave GameChanger and are moved into one of the company's divisions or to Shell Technology Ventures.

Similarly, a BCG report (2013) discussed the five factors that lead to strength in innovation: the commitment of senior management, the ability to leverage intellectual property (IP), a customer focus, strong management of the innovation portfolio, and well-defined and governed processes. These key aspects are visible in most innovative companies. An organized way of embedding them into practice is to follow a systematic deployment that can create not only long term but high impact innovations. This works because the BCG (2014) research also reported that world class companies treat innovation as a system. At the same time, another observation of this research is also that that many companies still suffer from a cautious culture, misguided incentives, and fearful decision-making and governance. Truly then, guiding points for organizations are to create strong environments where employees are treated as creative minds, and organizations should make realistic investments to support the development of ideas into successful innovation initiatives. This indeed requires adequate backing from leadership and a conducive culture to take calculated risks as well as guidance to turn the challenges into opportunities. This should function like a system and should develop as a culture for an organization to succeed. In this way, risk-taking is not a one-time or on/off behavior, but requires institutionalization of the same in its employees by carving strategies and policies for the creation of such an atmosphere.

SAP is another world leader—the third largest software house with a forty-five-year history of business innovation. It has 131 innovation and development centers across the globe and it has design thinking integrated into their business. They perceive design thinking as an innovation tool. Their simple way of solving problems is based on customer empathy. SAP leaders realized they needed to focus innovation back on customers. They built a business case for design thinking and it is deep rooted in everything they do.

One thing common among them is their approach to design thinking as their strategy to sustain innovation. Each company has a unique way of implanting design thinking into their organization's culture. Most innovative companies leverage emotions in finding the right problem. The focus is not just on generating ideas but also on finding better ideas.

In addition, the KPMG survey on the most innovative companies of the world, where Google takes the lead followed by Apple and IBM, reveals that global tech industry leaders believe the role of the Chief Information Officer (CIO) is best suited to lead the innovation strategy. Further, the survey reiterated that innovation incubation is no longer just the role of R&D. In fact, innovation is mostly spotted and nurtured in areas such as business units, strategic planning, information technology, etc. It's a fact that innovative companies have incorporated those behaviors into their routines.

Finally, another important aspect noted about the most innovative companies in the BCG research is that innovative companies think big, move fast, and are not afraid to fail. They put themselves through regular check-ups to make sure the system is working as it's supposed to.

So how do you elevate and leverage innovation status within your organization? In the next section, we will tackle the way to sustain those innovation efforts.

6.3 Sustaining Innovation

Our next question is how to bring innovation to life and sustain it? Challenges for sustaining innovation are multifold simply because the innovation output must also result in larger outcomes such as profitability, sustainability, governance, and particularly in larger public interest. There are several observation being made as to what outcomes are to be achieved out of innovation deployment. For example, the study by Klimentova (2014) more or less broadly describes outcomes as creating societal and environmental impacts, increasing quality, efficiency, and productivity, improved employee satisfaction, creates benefits for users, and brings about other intangible effects such as trust and legitimacy. These are not just the outcomes in the public interest but are also the key premises for a sustainable innovation as Savetpanuvong et al. (2011) concludes. Their study illustrates that concern for societal and environmental impacts, fair competition and equality of stakeholder treatment, as well as building long-term customer relationships with integrity, appropriate use of resources, diversification to reduce risk, and timely entrance into different market cycles, as several other impacts that innovation must target to achieve beyond the quick outputs such as new products or services or profit making. In order to strike a balance between outputs and outcomes (Savetpanuvong et al. 2011) highlights in an information technology context that organizations are needed to exploit innovation strategies through scale, scope, speed, superiority, and sustainability leading them for sustainable innovations. After all, innovation is not merely a technological issue but as a social and economic factor that is characteristically linked to the welfare of the people and to that of generations to come (Ali 2014). Several of these aspects bind us back to our 4C model in which each of these aspects are embedded. Given that challenges loom on the spectrum of achieving those broad outcomes, innovation deployment should follow a robust practice ensuring timely and effective outcomes. In doing so, the organization must build its organizational capability to achieve such long-term impact benefits. What actually drives those initiatives?

Research suggests that high-knowledge intensity and high visibility toward society appear to be the most favorable conditions for developing organizational capabilities leading to sustainable innovation (Ayuso 2011). And Thompson (2004) suggests that not everyone who starts an organization has the capability to be another Richard Branson or James Dyson, nor do they necessarily have the right temperament and motivation. People are the key sources of innovation in whom ideas rest. That being said, innovation labs are a huge trend in successful organizations. This is because idea labs enable organizations to stimulate and sustain innovation, ameliorating the hostility of corporate cultures to innovations (Narayanan 2017). Besides this, as Matser's (2010) research observed, appropriate attitudes, values, and norms on the part of top management are essential to developing a company culture that fosters innovation. This culture must then be supported by strategic methods and processes that further the uniqueness of the company.

Another big challenge facing innovation is that it has to be a risk worth taking, because ultimately the transformation of ideas has to result in viable new products (Thompson 2004). The focus suggested by researchers is also to proactively address common barriers such as risk aversion, which requires the monitoring of the portfolio of innovation projects and ensuring that high return projects are maintained even in the face of risks (Strategic Direction 2008).

No doubt understanding clearly the innovation barriers provides another avenue for sustaining innovation. The research of Adebisi SA and Babatunde on innovation management and organization development in the Nigerian banking system proposed the following insights:

- The organization should maintain continuous and effective research and development, and allow its entire staff to act as agents of change by giving them an equal and free hand in which to operate. This will increase the level of innovatory and organization growth.
- The organization should strictly adhere to the innovation management policy to achieve its vision, since it has been revealed that a company's market growth is a measure of its innovativeness.
- The organization should create adequate environment and social responsibilities as one of their objectives.

- All firms in the industry should consider the acquisition of modern technology a priority so as to improve their operation. It is revealed that the average customer would like to bank with innovative banks. If any company wants to achieve the purpose of its establishment, it must be up to date with technology and innovation.
- All firms in the industry should form an alliance and embark on a research and development project that will help improve and widen their operation in the industry.

Given that innovation results from a complex process, combining curiosity, creativity, rigorous scientific method, and a suitable institutional framework of interaction (Sener and Schepers 2017) is indeed is a key forward for sustaining innovation. Truly, the emergence of novel concepts or processes, products, or services can only result from out-of-the-box thinking, improvisation, trial and error, and new tacit or explicit knowledge (Gretschmann and Schepers 2016). On the contrary, Chesbrough (2003) highlights that most key inventions and innovations come from large corporate laboratories. This implies that opportunities for innovation exists in every organization and have only have to be nurtured for its success through its people. This can be achieved through good communication between individuals, departments, and companies as some form of collaboration describes most forms of innovation (Strategic Direction 2011).

A key message to sustain innovation is to build around following the directions:

Increase organization immunity to innovation discovery process through employees: One starting point to leverage the peoples' creativity is to begin asking questions—How are our people are absorbing innovation currently? Have they been able to capture their creativity freely? Innovation discovery is rooted in people having good ideas and good ideas are the results from learning from their failure. Hence people have to participate actively in the innovation pursuit. But the challenge is that corporates are not very willing to risk failures; on a practical level they want less risk. Many organizations indeed are immune to or have a limited tolerance for product or service failure, although the innovation is the result of many such failures in past attempts. In this manner of sustaining innovation, organizations should develop a balanced view for failure tolerance and employee's contracts should be amended in such a way that they don't back out on inculcating risk-taking behaviors. Particularly, depending on how people feel valued within their organization, they will tend to take a risk or make a decision to actively participate. It is a natural desire or human need to look for inclusion. When such inclusion is felt, people develop a desire for the pursuit of knowledge and are willing to take risks in the pursuit of knowledge. The desire for the pursuit of knowledge keeps people continuously thinking. Furthermore, when their fear is driven out and when they don't fear rejection they develop the ability to express themselves freely. The success measures of the organization can also be monitored through the volume of past failures. These volumes should be proportionate to the number of competencies or recognized innovators within the organizations. When the ratio is low, individuals need to be equipped with further training and tools to increase their innovation competency. Management must strike a balance that allows employees to act on good ideas (Brooke Dobni 2008). The key to ignite employees into innovation is to get them to participate, ensuring a feeling of inclusion by giving them their due importance in their roles and jointly building their competencies for their functional roles and taking care of their personal interests.

Involve everyone and unleash creativity at all levels: Innovation it is not a game involving just a few in the organization, nor it is to be executed only from the top although leaders are privy to success. The balance is in making the innovation function both from the top-down as well as from the top-up, as the innovation coach Govidarajan Rajan suggests in his interview with Brian Leavy for Strategic Directions (2011). He suggests that innovation should be both top-down and bottom-up. Setting up the right organizational architecture should be top-down (Leavy 2011). The innovation execution should be bottom-up. All employees, regardless of status or position, need to contribute. Employee constituency defines how employees think of themselves vis-a-vis the organization and their colleagues. For example, do they feel that they can contribute? Are they heard? Do they feel valued and equitably treated? Do they trust and respect management? Do they resonate with what the organization is doing—its mission and vision? Do they know what is important? And is there tension or fluidity in the day-to-day operations? It may be the case in some organizations that people are told to innovate, but they are not given the processes and tools they need to succeed. These are typically the ones who cannot proceed to innovation maturity.

Effective innovation process: According to Loewe and Dominiquini (2006), a good innovation process should have the capability to:

- Ensure that the new ideas generated aren't simply a re-hash of what has been done before.
- Synthesize individual ideas into bigger platforms before selecting individual ideas to develop further.
- Use experiments to test critical assumptions and refine the business model before locking it in.
- Adjust evaluation criteria throughout the process to reflect the stage of development of the innovation.

As the organization grows larger communications gets more complex, and hence leaders have to understand the organization's culture inside out, facilitate a relatively flat organization structure focusing on efficiency, and institute share leadership cross functional units.

Reward, compensation and celebration: Another important aspect to focus upon is to increase innovation capability through awareness of the customer and awareness of possible opportunities. Organizations should master this ability. Leaders have to ensure that they increase both external focus on the customer and internal focus on their systems.

Collaborative design from functional structures: Organizations must clearly motivate their employees and this motivation should proceed in a way that employees can naturally absorb the creative culture. Creating success stories is one crucial step in such successful deployments. Organizations should announce the success and make everyone aware of the innovation success. Ultimately it helps in sustaining the idea momentum for a long time (Hivner et al. 2003). A continuous flow of ideas increases the innovation funnel but also can ignite the success of one or two long-term initiatives adding to project portfolios. Given that R&D is not the only place for innovation to occur, due importance is to be given in creating a broader awareness of the need for innovation, and for communicating those successes to the employees in order for them to change from their traditional work behaviors to risk-taking behaviors, and more importantly, not taking on "following" roles but "leading" roles.

Understaffing customer experience and design thinking: Understanding customer experience is another big source of innovation. Co-creating leads to information sharing. J&J has a unique program on collaborating with customers and dealing with open-ended problems. Design Thinking (DT) is a mindset; it has moved from a buzz word to business strategy. DT is a tool for innovation which is deployed by many companies such as GE, SAP, and Dodge telecom. The CEOs of most these companies have attended a DT boot camp. The DT boot camp experience has helped those companies to transform their culture to DT. DT can be used as a designated function like other functional areas. When the value of this is experienced, then the entire organization will be willing to opt for it.

Embrace the barriers: One way to manage sustainable innovation is to understand the barriers fully. A research study of Das et al. (2018) identified a number of key internal barriers from eight different innovation projects within large multinational bank in Europe. These include: "a lack of exploiting new ideas," "inertia caused by (local) systems architecture," "an unsupportive organizational structure," "too much focus on risk avoidance," "absence of fundamental research and development," and "the not-invented-here-syndrome." Similarly, De Martino and Magnotti (2017) identified these obstacles as:

- the presence of uncertain demand;
- a market dominated by competitors;
- the difficulty of finding partners for innovation;
- lack of information about the market;
- lack of information on available technologies;
- lack of qualified staff;
- high innovation costs;
- lack of external sources of finance;
- lack of internal resources.

So for mastering the dynamics of innovation, a sustainable innovation engine is to be created. Strategy activity is the most necessary form of and the foundation for innovation. Without strategy, there is no motivation to innovate (Stewart and Fenn 2006). To conclude, one can introduce a strategy of the sustainable innovation engine based on multiple theories such as stakeholder theory, a resource-based view, a knowledge-based view, AMO, and the TQM approach which have all been linked and researched in the context of innovation and have found substantial positive relationships.

From the Resource-Based View (RBV) perspective, people and their knowledge are the building blocks from which new knowledge can be created (Milton Correia de Sousa 2006). From a knowledge perspective it is said that, as new knowledge resulting from innovation is fed back into the organization it results in creating a sustainable innovation engine (Milton Correia de Sousa 2006) and a disruption theory can be used to create a more-nearly balanced portfolio of innovative initiatives (Raynor 2011).

6.4 A Theoretical Framework for the Sustainable Innovation Engine

In this section, we will explore the relevance of each of these theories in proposing a sustainable innovation engine. Based on the above theories, sustainable innovation can be conceptualized as shown in Fig. 6.1.

The relevance of RBV theory to innovation: The resource-based theory (RBT) explains that the diverse resources owned by each organization differentiate an organization's performance levels and provide competitive advantage to the organization (Barney 1991). In the innovation context, for example technology, people, IT, and finance are all treated as organizational resources which have an impact on innovation deployment. Moreover, the resource-based theory has been examined in the context of innovation. For example, a study of Henard and McFadyen (2012) tracks the resource dedication and new product financial performance of forty-one firms over a seven-year period. They provide evidence that financial

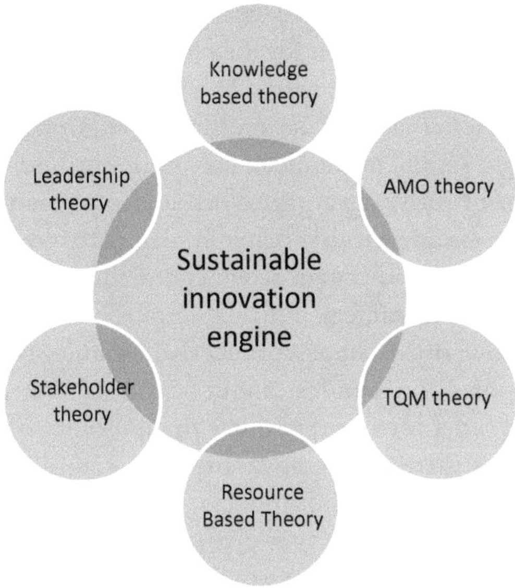

Fig. 6.1 Sustainable innovation engine

investments have a contemporaneous return on investment while knowledge worker investments provide companies with both contemporaneous and carryover returns. So they propose that when formulating strategy and making resource allocation decisions, managers must remain cognizant of the time-dependent nature of resource investments, the need for persistent investment, and the resulting performance impact. Moreover, RBV further explains that there are four empirical indicators of the potential of firm resources to generate competitive advantage: value, rareness, imitability, and substitutability. Lai et al. (2009) agreed that innovation need not be a totally new concept to the world and could even be considered an imitation of something already used elsewhere, but new to the unit of adoption. This implies that by imitating resources capability to a new context innovation can emerge in the everyday life of the organization. The digital platforms can add value to leverage each of the resources to achieve an optimal value and a substantial growth in digital platforms, purportedly energizing innovation. In fact, there is strong avocation that these digital resources can deliver and trigger innovation (Kleis et al. 2012). Given that the main foundation for the resource-based view of the firm is that the "type, magnitude, and nature of a firm's resources and capabilities are important determinants of its profitability" (Amit and Schoemaker 1991, p. 35), these should be moulded for sustaining innovation. Similarly, the firm has a competitive advantage when it is implementing a value creating strategy not simultaneously being implemented by competitors and a sustained competitive advantage when competitors are unable to duplicate the benefits of the strategy. Further, resources must be valuable to a firm to be a source of sustained competitive advantage and at the same time it must be rare. The resource cannot be easily imitated by competing firms. Finally, in order for a firm resource to be a source of sustained competitive advantage, there can be no strategically equivalent resources that themselves are not also rare and imitable. So resources such as increased technology or a digital platform may give increased technology innovation thereby contributing to new revenue or new strategy deployment resulting in a different type of organizational innovation. Moreover, Chen and Chen (2013) propose that if a firm can produce novel products or services by optimally utilizing its resources, its operating costs will decrease and additional external valuable resources or funding will accumulate. These effects will result in an increase in competitive advantages and will reduce a firm's dependence on external resources; as a result, the firm will succeed in constructing a barrier against its competitors. More interestingly, a review of the strategic management of organizational innovation (Keupp et al. 2012) has shown that the topic of "resources" plays a major role and that almost 50 percent of the 223 reviewed empirical papers employed resource-related independent variables. Truly, the dynamic nature of business activities requires firms to continuously extend their internal resources to innovate and create new competitive advantages (Cockburn et al. 2000). The literature on general innovation also has claimed that dynamic capabilities enable organizational innovation (e.g. Elkins and Keller 2003).

To sustain the innovation engine therefore, organizational dynamic capabilities such as resources must be viewed from the RBV, which suggests that resources must be have value, be rare, not easily imitability, and ensure substitutability.

Embedding such views to a sustainable innovation engine framework should pose the questions:

- Do we have valuable resources? What are we doing to increase the value of our resources?
- Are our resources rare? How do implicate these elements in our resources?
- Are our resources easily imitable? How do we make them unique to our services?

So from a theoretical perspective, a relation between innovation and RBV is accepted, especially when the influence of resources on innovation is considered. However, not enough empirical studies have been made regarding the various type of relations of resources to different dimensions of innovations and even fewer have been carried out regarding an influence in the opposite direction, that is, from innovation to resource practices. Future studies considering the relation between innovation and resources could perhaps analyze the type of innovation applied among firms using specific resources in order to determine whether their innovation is focused on social aspects, with a view to finding which aspects would be most relevant for obtaining competitive advantages or shareholder value creation.

The stakeholder theory: Much has been said about the importance of managing stakeholder relationships for gaining competitive advantage. Stakeholder theory helps companies understand the environment and the different constituents which managers should satisfy in order to effectively manage the organization (Agnete Alsos et al. 2011). Stakeholder theory represents a view which expects a value creation for a wider group of stakeholders. The innovation literature has also shown interest in a diverse range of stakeholders. Open innovation, user innovation (von Hippel 2009), co-creation (Kazadi et al. 2016; Prahalad and Ramaswamy 2004) and co-innovation (Lee et al. 2012) require business firms to be more open to collaboration with both primary and secondary stakeholders, because it is not always clear which stakeholders might possess the necessary knowledge. Primary stakeholders have been acknowledged as potential sources of innovation, with knowledge providers ranging from suppliers (Li and Vanhaverbeke 2009; Schiele 2010) to customers (Joshi and Sharma 2004), to consultants (Gemünden et al. 1996), and even to competitors (Lim et al. 2010).

Given that multiple stakeholders are involved in co-creation for innovation (Kazadi et al. 2016; Ramaswamy and Gouillart 2010), it is imperative that innovation has a strong basis for engaging with its specific stakeholders strategically. Going forward, a new collaborative innovation paradigm could increasingly require proactive stakeholder roles, as suggested by Lee et al. (2012).

Specifically, Harris (2010) illustrates that firms that manage for stakeholders develop trusting relationships, and stakeholders are more likely to share nuanced information regarding their utility functions, thereby increasing the ability of the firm to allocate its resources to areas that will best satisfy them. In addition, this information can spur innovation, as well as allowing the firm to deal better with changes in the environment. Moreover, the competitive advantages stemming from a "managing-for-stakeholders" approach are argued to be sustainable because they are associated with path dependency and causal ambiguity.

These explanations provide a strong rationale for including stakeholder theory in the discussion of managing innovation through the effective engagement of its stakeholders. Given that customer co-development and co-creation is at the center of innovation, so is the need to embrace other engagements such as partnerships, and external exchanges in extracting and nourishing those ideas to develop a pipeline for ideas and eventually the innovation portfolios. Embedding these explanations, stakeholder engagement of a firm must guide to identify high impact relationships that drive innovation. Moreover, the stakeholder relationships for the collaborative initiative are complex, involving multiple stakeholders with varying interests and goals (Savage 2011). In order to manage the sustainable innovation engine, organizations should understand the inputs that are to be captured through its important stakeholder engagement.

- Specifically, how are we engaging our stakeholders?
- What roles do they play in co-creation, co-development?
- How impactful have been the open innovations when engaging with the stakeholder groups?

Bringing the effective stakeholder perspective and managing those stakeholder expectations through co-development and co-creation would be one way of sustaining the innovation engine. We enhance a collaborative perspective of stakeholder theory, finding that stakeholders can play highly collaborative and proactive roles.

Future research can thus envisage how organizations can apply leverage from stakeholder proactive roles to respond to their demands of how the expectations of those stakeholders influence ongoing innovations in firms' products and services. Will conflicting stakeholder expectations contribute more to the challenges of fostering innovations?

6.4.1 Knowledge-Based View

The knowledge-based view is that new product creativity is primarily a function of a firm's ability to manage, maintain, and create knowledge (Gannt 1996). Basically, knowledge represents itself in the form of information and know-how, and a firm's ability to create and transfer this knowledge can yield competitive differentiation (Kogut and Zander 1992). As such, knowledge therefore can be constructed, and appropriate processes need to be in place in order to do so. Moreover, theory also points out an assumption that knowledge resides and is applied at the individual level (Harvey et al. 1999). KBV, which builds upon the resource-based view, considers knowledge as a very important business strategic resource (Conner 1991). Knowledge-based resources accumulated through organizational learning are usually difficult to develop or imitate and are often socially complex (Punnakitikashem et al. 2010).

In order to sustain the innovation engine, drawing from the knowledge-base view of the firm, the value of knowledge transfer activities is to be analyzed to understand when and how knowledge transfer is most effective and what practices are conducive to maintain this momentum. Knowledge, which resides in an individual, is amplified into organizational knowledge through an interactive process (Takeuchi 2013). Overall, an effective integration of the knowledge sharing into innovation process is warranted. Rightly, knowledge management is crucial for the innovation process (Powell 1996). So linking knowledge transfer and its management for successful innovation is indeed important. Accordingly, in the context of innovation, process management knowledge sharing is widely portrayed as key to the success of innovation management. Particularly, the ability to acquire and use knowledge is of central importance for innovating and improving performance. Moreover, the internal sources of information as well as external exchanges become privy in managing the organization.

Given that knowledge enables the development of core competencies, and enables firms to weather challenges, manage complexities, and remain competitive (Blome et al. 2014), there is a great potential for innovation deployment to benefit from this knowledge transfer. Also, as KBV suggests, firms should be analyzed based on their knowledge resources (Grant 1996). It is imperative that innovation assessment entails this is one of the indicators in our framework that we discussed in Chap. 4. A study of Gopalakrishnan and Bierly (1997) suggests that innovations that are based on tacit and systemic knowledge—as compared to those based on explicit and autonomous knowledge—are more likely to provide a sustainable source of competitive advantage. For innovations that are primarily based on tacit and systematic knowledge, the benefits are higher and costs lower if they are internally sourced. This type of knowledge is more likely to lead to competitive advantage since it is difficult to imitate and the firm's knowledge base will be expanded only if organizational members "experience" the knowledge. So, the "knowledge-based view" can be a useful framework in order to develop in an effective way firm innovations (Díaz-Díaz et al. 2008). Given that a firm capable in knowledge acquisition, knowledge dissemination, and responsiveness to knowledge is more innovative (Darroch 2005), the organization should leverage this aspect to foster continuous innovation.

So an obvious question to address and understand is: To what extent, and how, does knowledge exchange facilitate continuous and improving business outcomes? How, as an organization, can a framework for managing the internal and external knowledge exchange be managed? Are there conducive process that aim at appropriate exploitation of knowledge sharing and transfer?

6.4.2 Leadership Theory

Research has shown a link between the leadership style and innovation performance of an organization and hence there is need for emphasis on leadership for innovative performance. Effective leadership is integral for the capability of an organization to be creative and innovative. Over the years, scholars have investigated the relationship between various leadership theories and individual creativity and innovative behavior. Leaders' actions can be largely drawn from leadership theories. For example, transformational leadership helps to stimulate idea generation (Kahai et al. 2003) Khalili (2016) documented that transformational leaders positively and significantly influence employees' creativity and innovation. Authentic leaders further their followers' trust, respect, and identification (Avolio et al. 2004; Ilies et al. 2005), enabling them to suggest new and fresh thoughts and to feel free to take risks and to propose contradictory beliefs without fear (Walumbwa et al. 2010). Many of the risk-taking leaders easily lead the way by being an example and eventually employees become bold and fearless (McGing and Brown 2014).

Particularly, the leadership's role has to do with creating an environment where imagination, smart risk-taking, aggressive initiatives, and bold tactics are encouraged and rewarded. Research further suggests that in order for these Small Medium Enterprises (SMEs) to emerge and succeed within the global ranks, an innovative leadership with the willingness to take calculated risks is required (Maladzhi 2015). A recent study of Dodge reveals that there are fundamental leadership dimensions that can influence how innovative an organization's employees perceive it to be. According to this study, the three most important leadership dimensions for innovation are organizational encouragement, challenging work, and work group support. Given that creativity and innovation can be used as important tools to fuel corporate growth (Baker et al. 2016), leaders have a very influential role to play.

Given the importance of leadership for effective innovation deployment, good practices for leadership must be drawn from supportive leadership theories that guide the risk-taking behaviors among employees that are key for sustaining the innovation engine.

Finally, the relevance of TQM and AMO theory is already discussed in Chap. 2. Both of these theories support the various components of the 4C model. The organizational capability and people enabler can be embraced from the AMO perspective. The TQM theory also suggest strong linkages to innovation practice. While incremental innovations are a clear result of quality improvement, by embracing people and customer oriented practices, the organizational element can elevate ways of co-creation and co-development profoundly.

The conceptual framework provides several avenues for future research particularly for strengthening the innovation engine. Practices must not only evolve but must remain modern and relevant! In the next section we will discuss some of the future avenues that would be of interest to keep the innovation engine alive!

6.4.3 Future Research: Continuous Innovation

In this chapter, we have derived a detailed guideline for sustaining the innovation engine alongside a 4C model framework for assessing innovation in organizations as a basis for achieving continuous innovation performance. This framework is different from other frameworks as it mainly helps the organization to carry out a self-assessment and improve upon its innovation journey. In this framework, we are first focusing on the elaboration of the leadership component and discuss the indicators to ascertain the leadership support needed for a successful deployment. Second, we focus on the people aspect of innovation alongside the necessary indicators to be assessed and finally, we elaborate on the organizational capability. Organizational capability-building is crucial for sustained innovation and hence we identify several aspects that are to be well-tuned for a successful innovation deployment. We discuss the innovation outcomes that are to be achieved when the innovation enablers are well supported. We envisage that a clearer picture on each of the enablers with its respective exhibits will significantly add to the overall innovation performance of the organization. Furthermore, integrating the concept of perceived barriers for innovation helps to better understand the obstacles that hinder innovation performance. Organizations may have set the right direction by pulling on the innovation levers, but there may be some hindrances which can stall the innovation process. Particularly, these hindrances may occur organically as the organization expands and faces other business challenges. So herein, a clearer picture on each of the effects emerging from the dynamic environments must be studied in relation to the theories that base our innovation enablers.

Moreover, it is vital to understand the contextual and environmental difference factors that affect each of these enablers and hinder the innovation performance. Although innovative organizations shed light on what works and what does not, further research in this respect is hampered, as long as there is no clarity on potentially useful innovative initiatives existent in the organization when barriers are taken into consideration. Based on the fundamental notion that it is not possible for an organization to function always in the same style, given the dynamics around it are continually changing, a better understanding of the antecedents that lead organizational members to engage in either form of innovation response behavior is therefore of utmost interest.

Answers to these questions will provide the important impetus and starting points for managerial and organizational influence, such as organizational support for innovation. This will further enhance our understanding of the respective behaviors associated with role model concepts, allowing for a closer examination and unfolding what leads to more or less innovative performance. A better understanding of the resulting action modes of enablers will help managers and organizational leaders to better support enablers and watch out for the barriers in the innovation deployment. Given that the nature of innovation is highly complex, the stakeholder-based view of the organizational innovation process seems a promising way for future research to understand how to engage stakeholders for an optimal output. This understanding can profoundly influence partnerships management, networking, and knowledge sharing for managing innovations. What are the new ways of engaging with partnerships and what will continue strategic partnership that will bring about high impact innovation, and what supports an organization's ongoing endeavours?

Similarly, a deep contribution is possible in relation to various theories. Sustainable innovation can be studied in light of various theories such as stakeholder management because stakeholder relations are quite crucial. A study was done to prove that engagement with different stakeholders is a valid mechanism for promoting sustainable innovation within firms (Ayuso et al. 2011). As such, many of the difficulties associated with the stirring up of employees' imagination capital can be directly related to the management of knowledge (Brooke Dobni 2008). Similarly, innovation can be studied in light of RBV theory to understand the management of resource implications for innovation. Such integration of theories is important mainly because a firm may be able to access useful knowledge located in diverse stakeholder's groups, but not enhance its innovation if it does not have enough capacity to absorb such new knowledge and integrate it into its innovation processes (Ayuso 2011). Further, because, "value-creating opportunities" are best identified by observing and understanding the relevant business cluster: the industry, competitors and customers, as described by (Brooke Dobni 2008), this provides an impetus for integrating knowledge management theory to integrate knowledge sharing practices that provide guidance to capitalize on this aspect for sustainable innovation. RBV researchers find roots to innovation linkages to IT resources, and future research can also address the best practices to foster the linkages between technology and various dimension of innovation. From a theoretical perspective, a relation between innovation and RBV is accepted, especially when the influence of resources on innovation is considered. However, not enough empirical studies have been made regarding the various type of relations of resources to different dimensions of innovations and even fewer have been carried out regarding an influence in the opposite direction, that is, from innovation to resource practices.

Future studies considering the relation between innovation and resources could perhaps analyze the type of innovation applied among firms using specific resources in order to determine whether their innovations are focused on social aspects, with a view to finding which aspects would be most relevant for obtaining competitive advantages or shareholder value creation. It would also be interesting to examine whether particular internal or external determinants at multiple levels primarily affect innovation inputs or outputs. On this basis, future work may identify some determinants that are positively related to multiple innovation types, whereas others positively affect one type, for example service innovation, and negatively influence another type, for example management innovation. Here, the role of moderators at multiple levels may play an important role. With these observation, some of the key propositions that would be of interest to address in future research are: People aspects—What and how do we continue to engage creative minds to leverage the innovation in complex and difficult situations? How do we protect people's ideas from abuse and exploitation? How can organizations exploit the right ideas for high-impact innovation? Are there any implications for Human Resources (HR) practice? Do we need a code for creative minds engagement? People moreover have to be motivated for taking risks, so how can we leverage this aspect and what implication does it have for HR practice for innovation management? Partnerships and Collaborative Places—How is the pooling-in of resources and creative places shaping up to produce a high-impact innovation? How can small firms and industries leverage from these collaborative places? What does this imply for small scale organizations?

Overall, as much as continuous innovation becomes a challenge, organizations need ways for sustaining their growth innovation asset. Rightly as innovation is a strategic resource for organizations, future research will have to focus on several aspects of managing this innovation engine. Future research on innovation therefore requires attention at micro as well as macro levels. Although we have developed a good understating of various levers fostering innovation and great frameworks and strategic agendas that have helped organizations as well as nations to take advantage of innovation, more has to be done to learn how to sustain the momentum of innovation and how to lead this wave on to continuous innovation. Some of these emerging agendas are as follows:

Dimensions of measurements: Given that innovation outcomes are crucial and organizations should aim at high-impact innovation as well to create a social benefit, assessment of innovation will always be an ongoing research agenda. In previous studies, it has been observed that measuring the effects that innovative activities have on productivity and growth is an area of active research (Hall et al. 2009; Tether and Howells 2007). However, due to the variability and uncertainty inherent in innovation, determining the magnitude of the effect remains elusive. Service innovation is increasingly seen as a vector of sustainable growth and competitive advantage at the firm-, industry- and economy-level. With the increasing growth of services in today's organizations and economy, the importance of understanding the service innovation concepts and practices is also on the rise. Future research should also address a development of measurement aiming at service innovations. The process of innovation must be viewed as a series of changes in a complete system not only of hardware but also of market environment, production facilities, and the knowledge and social context of the innovation organization (Kline and Rosenerg 1986).

Ultimately, however, it is the innovation orientation of top management as well as its leadership skills that are the true sources of competitive advantage (Matzlers 2001). As leaders pose as strong contributors to innovation challenge, a research area emerging in this direction is to understand what it takes to lead innovation organization and innovation economy. How does the ecosystem of innovation becomes privy to leaders' attention given the global challenges keep looming?

A strong pillar for our framework which is frequently mentioned in the literature is organizational capability. Although good practices relating to each of these are evolving, are unique, and crucial to innovation, future research tabulating these to create standards for leveraging each of the capability indicators would also be beneficial. Particularly, given that knowledge generation, innovation, and ultimately value creation will increasingly be located outside the boundaries of a single firm (Ayuso 2011) a study of highbred collaborative arrangements and frameworks can be great source for sustaining innovations. We cannot discount the value and key role that technology has played in facilitating this, but there will always be a need to grow this interconnection space beyond technology connections.

Finally, integrating antecedents from different theoretical models, we have shown how to influence innovation performance and suggested a theoretically founded framework that includes good practices and is a guide to future research in innovation management.

In sum, we believe that identifying the influence of the different enablers on the innovation deployment under dynamic scenarios and how it affects the innovation projects is an interesting area for further research. Further, to embrace the complexity of innovation practices, a basic to mature level of standardization would help the managers in the organization to set out on innovation deployment at ease.

6.5 Conclusion

Innovation is considered an important factor for global competition and it is perfectly fine for organizations to embrace innovation. However, the path for moving into innovation is not easy. Of particular difficulty is that an organization may end up in frustration and failure if innovation is unsuccessful. This requires a firm basis for organizations to set their innovation foundation right by developing employees who need to have more than average competencies to innovate, leadership who can set strategic directions and guide risk-taking behaviors and develop dynamic organizational capabilities based on sound theories for innovation management. The most innovative companies therefore view innovation not only as a system but also assess and measure their innovation deployments. Organizations should invest and develop their innovation capabilities as discussed in the 4C model of innovation assessment.

Truly reaching the top list on the innovation ladder is one challenge, sustaining that performance is another equally important challenge and hence to be successful, sustainability of the initiative must be embedded in the process of innovation from the beginning. Starting right and doing right from the first should be a new slogan for innovation. Continuous innovation is possible only when the organization invests in sustainable practices that take an organization a long way. The themes that we have suggested are quite important for a deep-rootedness in the innovation DNA of the organization.

Finally, future research scenarios guided by various theories can help us develop an innovation sustainable engine. One such model proposed in this chapter can be a starting point which argues the importance of integrating several of the theories that are already contributing to the innovation drive. The engine proposed here has several implications for empirically testing these in different sectors and proposing theoretical contributions extending the various theories. A combination of pursuing both first-mover and fast-follower strategies is encouraged to sustain innovation (Savetpanuvong et al. 2011). The need for critical transformation of people with ideas into effective entrepreneurs should be the focus of the future for sustaining innovation and has already been proposed (Thompson 2004), however actions have to be put in place to make it effective. For example, 3M is able to spread ideas because it encourages people to network. The organization deliberately fosters innovation through people by offering every employee the opportunity to spend 15 percent of their work time developing fresh ideas they have.

In the future, we may also need studies to advance our understanding on firms' sustainable innovation processes by framing this phenomenon as an organizational capability. In general, we can suggest that future attention should be on the standardization of innovation practices to be tuned to risk-taking behaviors. Innovation practices are needed for building and sustaining risk-taking behaviors. This is because a smooth and seamless innovation culture requires organizational encouragment for strong risk-taking behavior from individual employees of the organization. If companies are capable of combining access and transformation of relevant stakeholder information through specific routines, these organizational capabilities will confer on them a sustained competitive advantage (Ayuso 2011).

Finally, it is a challenging world out there, and it is only continuous innovation that guarantees the survival and sustainability of not only a business organization, but also the social and community-oriented developments. If innovation is not just about creating something entirely new, then what stops one to think and act innovatively? What stops us from embracing change for the bettering and impacting of our lives?

References

Agnete Alsos, Gry, Ulla Hytti, and Elisabet Ljunggren. 2011. Stakeholder Theory Approach to Technology Incubators. *International Journal of Entrepreneurial Behavior & Research* 17 (6): 607–625.

Ali, Abbas J. 2014. Innovation, Happiness, and Growth. *Competitiveness Review* 24 (1): 2–4 https://doi.org/10.1108/CR-09-2013-0075.

Amit, R., and P.J. Schoemaker. 1991. Strategic Assets and Organizational Rent. *Strategic Management Journal* 14: 33–46.

Avolio, B.J., W.L. Gardner, F.O. Walumbwa, F. Luthans, and D.R. May. 2004. Unlocking the Mask: A Look at the Process by Which Authentic Leaders Impact Follower Attitudes and Behaviors. *The Leadership Quarterly* 15 (6): 801–823.

Ayuso, Silvia, Miguel Ángel Rodríguez, Roberto García-Castro, and Miguel Ángel Ariño. 2011. Does Stakeholder Engagement Promote Sustainable Innovation Orientation. *Industrial Management & Data Systems* 111 (9): 1399–1417 https://doi.org/10.1108/02635571111182764.

Baker, W.E., A. Grinstein, and N. Harmancioglu. 2016. Whose Innovation Performance Benefits More from External Networks: Entrepreneurial or Conservative Firms? *Journal of Product Innovation Management* 33 (1): 104–120.

Barney, J. 1991. Firm Resources and Sustained Competitive Advantage. *Journal of Management* 17 (1): 99–120.

BCG. 2018. https://www.bcg.com/publications/2018/most-innovative-companies-2018-how-digital-transforms-strategy.aspx

Blome, C., T. Schoenherr, and D. Eckstein. 2014. The Impact of Knowledge Transfer and Complexity on Supply Chain Flexibility: A Knowledge-Based View. *International Journal of Production Economics* 147: 307–316.

Brooke Dobni, C. 2008. The DNA of Innovation. *Journal of Business Strategy* 29 (2): 43–50 https://doi.org/10.1108/02756660810858143.

Chen, Jui-Kuei, and I-Shuo Chen. 2013. A Theory of Innovation Resource Synergy. *Innovations* 15 (3): 368–392.

Cockburn, I.M., R.M. Henderson, and S. Stern. 2000. Untangling the Origins of Competitive Advantage. *Strategic Management Journal* 21 (10–11): 1123–1145.

Conner, K. 1991. A Historical Comparison of Resource-Based Theory and Five Schools of Thought Within Industrial Economics: Do We Have a New Theory of the Firm? *Journal of Management* 17 (1): 121–154.

Correia de Sousa, M. 2006. The Sustainable Innovation Engine. *Vine* 36 (4): 398–405.

Das, Patrick, Robert Verburg, Alexander Verbraeck, and Lodewijk Bonebakker. 2018. Barriers to Innovation Within Large Financial Services Firms: An In-Depth Study into Disruptive and Radical Innovation Projects at a Bank. *European Journal of Innovation Management* 21 (1): 96–112.

De Martino, Marcella, and Fabio Magnotti. 2017. The Innovation Capacity of Small Food Firms in Italy. *European Journal of Innovation Management* https://doi.org/10.1108/EJIM-04-2017-0041. Permanent link to this document: https://doi.org/10.1108/EJIM-04-2017-0041.

Díaz-Díaz, N., I. Aguiar-Díaz, and P. DeSaá-Pérez. 2008. The Effect of Technological Knowledge Assets on Performance: The Innovation Choice in Spanish Firms. *Research Policy* 37: 1515–1529.

Elkins, T., and R.T. Keller. 2003. Leadership in Research and Development Organizations: A Literature Review and Conceptual Framework. *The Leadership Quarterly* 14 (4): 587–606.

Estelyiová, K., and O. Žižlavský. 2012. Boosting Innovation Through Interfirm-Cooperation. *Economics and management* 17 (4): 1564–1571.

Gopalakrishnan, S., and P. Bierly. 1997. Organizational Innovation and Strategic Choices: A Knowledge-Based View. *Academy of Management Proceedings* 1997 (1): 422–426 Briarcliff Manor, NY 10510: Academy of Management.

Grant, R.M. 1996. Toward a Knowledge-Based Theory of the Firm. *Strategic Management Journal, Winter Special Issue* 17: 109.

Gretschmann, K., and S. Schepers, eds. 2016. *Revolutionising EU Innovation Policy: Pioneering the Future*. Springer.

Harvey, M.G., C. Speier, and M.M. Novicevic. 1999. The Impact of Emerging Markets on Staffing the Global Organization: A Knowledge-Based View. *Journal of International Management* 5 (3): 167–186.

Henard, D.H., and M.A. McFadyen. 2012. Resource Dedication and New Product Performance: A Resource-Based View. *Journal of Product Innovation Management* 29 (2): 193–204.

Hivner, Walter, Willie E. Hopkins, and Shirley A. Hopkins. 2003. Facilitating, Accelerating, and Sustaining the Innovation Diffusion Process: An Epidemic Modeling Approach. *European Journal of Innovation Management* 6 (2): 80–89.

Ilies, R., F.P. Morgeson, and J.D. Nahrgang. 2005. Leadership and Eudaemonic Well-Being: Understanding Leader-Follower Outcomes. *The Leadership Quarterly* 16 (3): 373–394.

Joshi, A.W., and S. Sharma. 2004. Customer Knowledge Development: Antecedents and Impact on New Product Performance. *Journal of Marketing* 68 (4): 47–59.

Kahai, S.S., J.J. Sosik, and B.J. Avolio. 2003. Effects of Leadership Style, Anonymity, and Rewards on Creativity-Relevant Processes and Outcomes in an Electronic Meeting System Context. *The Leadership Quarterly* 14 (4/5): 499–524.

Kazadi, K., A. Lievens, and D. Mahr. 2016. Stakeholder Co-creation During the Innovation Process: Identifying Capabilities for Knowledge Creation Among Multiple Stakeholders. *Journal of Business Research* 69 (2): 525–540.

Keupp, M.M., M. Palmié, and O. Gassmann. 2012. The Strategic Management of Innovation: A Systematic Review and Paths for Future Research. *International Journal of Management Reviews* 14 (4): 367–390.

Khalili, A. 2016. Linking Transformational Leadership, Creativity, Innovation, and Innovation-Supportive Climate. *Management Decision* 54 (9): 2277–2293.

Kleis, L., et al. 2012. Information Technology and Intangible Output: The Impact of IT Investment on Innovation Productivity. *Information Systems Research* 23 (1): 42–59.

Klimentova, Sabina. 2014. Innovation in the Public Sector: Is It Measurable?. In *Performance Measurement and Management Control: Behavioral Implications and Human Actions*, 289–315. Published online: 13 Oct 2014. Permanent link to this document: https://doi.org/10.1108/S1479-351220140000028021.

Kogut, B., and U. Zander. 1992. Knowledge of the Firm, Combinative Capabilities, and the Replication Of Technology. *Organization Science* 3 (3): 383–397.

Lai, E.L.-C., R. Riezman, and P. Wang. 2009. Outsourcing of Innovation. *Economic Theory* 38 (3): 485–515.

Leavy, Brian. 2011. Vijay Govindarajan: Innovation Coach to the Developed and Developing World. *Strategy & Leadership* 39 (5): 4–12 https://doi.org/10.1108/10878571111161471.

Li, Y., and W. Vanhaverbeke. 2009. The Relationships Between Foreign Competition, Absorptive Capacity and Pioneering Innovation: An Empirical Investigation in Canada. *International Journal of Innovation Management* 13 (01): 105–137.

Loewe, Pierre, and Jennifer Dominiquini. 2006. Overcoming the Barriers to Effective Innovation. *Strategy & Leadership* 34 (1): 24–31 https://doi.org/10.1108/10878570610637858.

Maladzhi, W.R. 2015. Impact of Risk-Taking Leadership on Organisational Performance and Sustainability in SMEs. In *2015 IEEE International Conference on Industrial Engineering and Engineering Management (IEEM)*, pp. 1752–1756. IEEE.

McGing, S., and A. Brown. 2014. Actuaries Institute, Risk Culture Leadership, Measurement & Management – A Comparison across Industries, Financial Service Forum, 5–6 May 2014.

Narayanan, V.K. 2017. Idea Labs: Instituting an Innovation Discovery Process Capable of Sustaining the Business. *Strategy & Leadership* 45 (1): 27–36 https://doi.org/10.1108/SL-12-2016-0089. Permanent link to this document: https://doi.org/10.1108/SL-12-2016-0089.

Petkovska, T. 2015. The Role and Importance of Innovation in Business of Small and Medium Enterprises. *Economic Development/ekonomiski razvoj* 17: pp. 55–74.

Prahalad, C.K., and V. Ramaswamy. 2004. Co-creation Experiences: The Next Practice in Value Creation. *Journal of Interactive Marketing* 18 (3): 5–14.

Punnakitikashem, P., Somsuk, N., McLean, M.W. and Laosirihongthong, T. 2010. Linkage Between Continual Improvement and Knowledge-Based View Theory. In *2010 IEEE 17th International Conference on Industrial Engineering and Engineering Management (IE&EM)*, October, pp. 1689–1694. IEEE

Ramaswamy, V., and F. Gouillart. 2010. Building the Co-creative Enterprise. *Harvard Business Review* 88 (10): 100–109.

Raynor, Michael E. 2011. Disruption Theory as a Predictor of Innovation Success/Failure. *Strategy & Leadership* 39 (4): 27–30 https://doi.org/10.1108/10878571111147378. Permanent link to this document: https://doi.org/10.1108/10878571111147378.

Savetpanuvong, P., U. Tanlamai, and C. Lursinsap. 2011. Sustaining Innovation in Information Technology Entrepreneurship with a Sufficiency Economy Philosophy. *International Journal of Innovation Science* 3 (2): 69–82.

Schiele, H. 2010. Early Supplier Integration: The Dual Role of Purchasing in New Product Development. *R&d Management* 40 (2): 138–153.

Sener, S., and S. Schepers, eds. 2017. *Innovation, Governance and Entrepreneurship: How Do They Evolve in Middle Income Countries?* https://doi.org/10.1007/978-3-319-55926-1_1.

Stewart, Ian, and Peter Fenn. 2006. Strategy: The Motivation for Innovation. *Construction Innovation* 6 (3): 173–185 https://doi.org/10.1108/14714170610710703.

Strategic Direction. 2008. Reviewing Innovation Effort: Innovation Culture. *Strategic Direction* 24 (10): 32–34 https://doi.org/10.1108/02580540810907128.

———. 2011. Innovate or Die: Why Innovation Is the Key to Business Success in a Changing World. *Strategic Direction* 27 (7): 12–14 https://doi.org/10.1108/02580541111137010.

Takeuchi, Hirotaka. 2013. Knowledge-Based View of Strategy. *Universia Business Review* 40: 68–79.

Tether, B.S., and Howells, J. 2007. Changing Understanding of Innovation in Services: From Technological Adoption to Complex Complementary Changes to Technologies, Skills and Organisation.

Thompson, J.L. 2004. Innovation Through People. *Management Decision* 42 (9): 1082–1094.
Von Hippel, E. 2009. Democratizing Innovation: The Evolving Phenomenon of User Innovation. *International Journal of Innovation Science* 1 (1): 29–40.
Walumbwa, F.O., P. Wang, H. Wang, J. Schaubroeck, and B.J. Avolio. 2010. Psychological Processes Linking Authentic Leadership to Follower Behaviors. *The Leadership Quarterly* 21 (5): 901–914.

Index

A

Ability, 4, 6, 7, 12, 13, 15, 19, 25, 28, 35, 36, 41–45, 55, 61, 62, 64–66, 71–73, 75, 79, 82, 90, 143, 157, 160, 165, 166, 172–174
Advanced, 1, 20, 23, 78, 80–82, 91, 92, 95, 98, 101, 107, 109, 111–113, 152
AMO theory, 42, 176
Assessment, vi, 2, 25, 26, 35, 42, 51–82, 89, 106, 127–129, 131, 133, 136, 150, 156, 158, 174, 176, 179, 181
Assessment awards, 26, 127–128, 131, 136, 156
Awareness, 94, 103, 104, 116, 128, 141, 155, 166

B

Barriers, 163, 167, 170, 176, 177
Building motivations, 42, 63, 65, 79, 97, 99, 114

C

Capability-building, vi, 9, 43, 65–75, 79, 81, 82, 91, 99, 100, 102, 112, 118, 176
Co-creation, 55, 56, 60, 67, 79, 92, 93, 95, 96, 107, 112, 114, 118, 171–173, 176
Co-development, 60, 68, 72, 75, 80, 91, 92, 96, 105, 107, 110, 114, 117–118, 172, 173, 176
Collective imagination, 61, 64–65, 72, 77, 79, 97, 99, 106, 115

F. Lasrado, *Fostering Creativity and Innovation*,
https://doi.org/10.1007/978-3-319-99121-4

Communication, 9, 24, 25, 40, 44, 55, 58–60, 69, 73, 74, 79, 82, 93, 94, 96, 102, 107, 114, 128, 129, 138, 156, 164, 166
Creativity, v, vi, 1–28, 35–45, 52, 55–59, 61–64, 68, 69, 73, 75, 79, 89, 91, 95–104, 107, 108, 114, 115, 139, 142, 147, 150, 164, 173, 175
Culture, v, 1–28, 37, 51, 52, 54, 55, 57, 58, 60, 64, 66, 70, 73, 74, 76, 78, 79, 81, 82, 92, 93, 95, 96, 99, 100, 102–104, 108, 118, 127–130, 133, 137–139, 141–143, 145–147, 150, 156, 158–161, 163, 166, 167, 182
Customer focus, 37, 38, 41, 160

D

Deployment, vi, 2, 13–15, 22, 41, 43, 52, 60, 89–92, 94–96, 98, 101–103, 109, 113, 134, 135, 156, 158, 160, 162, 166, 168, 170, 174–177, 180, 181
Design thinking (DT), 10–13, 28, 55, 69, 161, 167
Developmental, 63, 80, 82, 91, 92, 94, 95, 101, 103, 105, 109, 111

E

Employee participation, 37, 55, 61, 62, 74, 82, 129
Enablers, 35, 51–54, 59, 65, 69, 72, 77–79, 81, 82, 91, 96, 99, 101, 103, 111–116, 119, 121, 135–136, 157, 176, 177, 180
Expertise, 62, 64, 65, 79, 82, 97, 99, 107, 114, 134, 142, 146

F

Financial resources, 75, 101
Fostering, v, 6–8, 10, 26, 35, 38, 39, 43, 51, 56, 57, 60, 62, 66, 72, 78, 79, 81, 82, 95, 112, 118, 127, 128, 133, 139, 145, 147, 149, 150, 156, 173, 174, 178, 179

G

Group work, 62

I

Ideas, 3–7, 9–13, 15, 17, 19, 21–25, 28, 36, 38, 40, 41, 44, 51, 55–65, 68–75, 79, 89, 90, 95–100, 102–107, 114, 115, 118, 128, 129, 137–139, 141, 144–147, 150, 153, 159–161, 163–167, 172, 175, 179, 181, 182
Ideation, 10–13, 73
Index, 16, 17, 19, 21, 105, 142
Initial, 9, 60, 64, 69, 78, 80, 82, 91, 92, 94, 97, 101, 103, 105, 109, 111, 112, 119, 121, 131, 136, 160

Innovation, 1–28, 35–45, 51–82, 89–182
Involvement, 12, 37, 40, 44, 55, 56, 60, 62, 64, 67, 79, 80, 82, 97–99, 107, 128

K

Knowledge-based theory, 45, 168, 173–174

L

Leadership, vi, 2, 8, 10, 18, 35–37, 40, 42, 43, 54–60, 79, 81, 90, 91, 97, 103, 107, 112, 113, 118, 134, 135, 137, 138, 141, 144, 146, 151, 161, 166, 175–176, 180, 181

M

Maturity, 78–82, 89–126, 129, 131, 135, 166
Motivation, v, 35, 39, 41–44, 54, 57, 62–65, 73, 97, 99, 104, 106–111, 114, 116, 163, 166, 168

N

Networking, 55, 58–60, 72, 79, 82, 93, 96, 107, 114, 128, 145, 146, 151, 177
New product, 3, 4, 36, 52, 64, 66, 71, 77, 104, 105, 110, 116, 117, 142, 152, 159, 160, 162, 163, 168, 173

O

Opportunity, v, 1, 9, 11, 19, 22, 25, 35, 41–44, 55, 57–58, 60, 64–66, 68, 69, 73, 75, 77, 79, 82, 93, 95, 96, 99, 101, 112, 113, 122, 128, 129, 131, 142, 145, 148, 150–151, 154, 161, 164, 166, 178, 182
Organizational support, 8, 10, 58, 63, 68, 79, 177
Outcomes, vi, 18, 35, 42–44, 51–54, 71, 75–78, 80–82, 90, 91, 95, 97, 98, 103–105, 107, 109, 110, 112, 124–125, 162, 174, 176, 179

P

Participation, 37, 42, 45, 53, 55, 56, 60–63, 67, 72, 74, 79, 82, 95–97, 99, 107, 114, 128, 129, 141, 146, 153, 164, 165
Partnerships, 64, 68, 71, 74, 75, 79, 91, 93, 95, 96, 100, 107, 114, 131, 136, 145, 146, 152, 172, 177, 179
People, vi, 8–12, 18, 35, 37, 38, 43, 44, 55, 57, 58, 61–65, 69, 79, 81, 82, 90, 91, 93–100, 102, 103, 105, 107, 110, 112, 114, 118, 119, 140, 146, 148, 162–166, 168, 176, 179, 181, 182
Places, 12, 20, 21, 23, 60, 66–70, 74, 75, 79, 82, 90–92, 99–106, 108, 110, 111, 113, 115, 118, 119, 133, 135, 138, 139, 166, 173, 179, 181

Practices, 6, 8–10, 12, 15, 19, 23, 35, 37–41, 45, 55, 57, 58, 64, 66, 67, 69–71, 74, 77–82, 90–92, 94, 96–99, 102–105, 107, 108, 113–115, 118, 120, 124–125, 129, 130, 133, 134, 139, 143–147, 151, 155, 156, 158, 160, 162, 171, 173, 175, 176, 178–182
Process, 2–4, 6, 7, 9–14, 20–22, 36–40, 45, 51–53, 58, 61, 63–70, 72, 74–82, 89–92, 94–96, 98–107, 109, 110, 113–115, 117–119, 128, 131–133, 135, 136, 138, 139, 141–143, 145, 149–153, 156–160, 163, 164, 166, 173, 174, 177, 178, 180–182

R

Recognition, 12, 43, 57, 62, 68, 73–75, 80, 98, 99, 103, 104, 108, 110–117, 129, 132, 133, 136, 138, 156
Relational co-creation, 56–57, 95, 96, 107, 114
Resource-based view (RBV), 168, 170
Resources, 2, 4, 6, 9, 15, 42, 44, 52, 54, 60–62, 66–69, 71, 72, 74, 75, 79, 80, 91, 93, 94, 96, 99–103, 106, 107, 114, 115, 143, 145, 150, 162, 167–173, 178, 179
Results, 3, 4, 6, 14, 15, 20, 25, 36, 37, 40–42, 45, 51–54, 61, 66, 71, 72, 75–78, 80–82, 89–91, 93, 95, 97, 100–102, 104, 105, 107, 113, 119, 129, 130, 132, 135–139, 153–155, 162–164, 168, 170, 176
Rewards, 10, 44, 62, 63, 68, 73–75, 98, 99, 103, 104, 108, 111, 116, 118, 130, 146, 160, 166, 175
Risk-taking, 81, 91, 99, 106, 147, 161, 165, 167, 175, 181, 182
Role models, 56, 60, 71, 81, 93–96, 107, 112, 114, 153, 177

S

Service development, 105, 110, 117–119
Stakeholder theory, 168, 171–173
Strategy, 8, 11, 14–18, 20, 21, 23, 25, 35, 39, 51, 52, 60, 66, 68, 70, 71, 73, 74, 76, 80, 91, 95–97, 99, 103, 104, 108, 116, 119, 129, 130, 133–135, 138, 139, 141–144, 147, 149, 153, 159–162, 167–170, 181
Success stories, 154, 166
Suggestions, 9, 12, 55, 59, 146, 150
Sustainable engine, 181
Sustainable innovation, vi, 2, 26, 162, 163, 167–173, 177, 178, 182

T

Teamwork, 37, 39–41, 64, 98, 118
Technology, 3, 14, 16, 18, 20, 22–24, 26, 28, 36, 39, 59, 66, 67, 69, 72, 76, 100, 101, 103,

106, 115, 130, 137, 139, 141, 143, 147, 149–151, 158, 160–162, 164, 167, 168, 170, 178, 180
Tools, vi, 9–13, 17, 18, 20, 21, 28, 37–41, 61, 69, 89–91, 97–99, 106–111, 114, 119, 129, 133, 134, 138, 147, 151, 156, 161, 165–167, 175
Top management support, 8, 10, 37
Total quality management (TQM), 35–45, 134, 168, 176
Training, 9, 40, 42, 44, 55, 64, 65, 79, 82, 96–99, 107, 114, 130, 141, 146, 151, 165

U

UAE Innovation Award, 19, 20, 127–131, 137, 142, 144, 149, 156
UAE innovation legacy, 17, 21–24
United Arab Emirates (UAE), 15–26, 127–131, 133, 134, 136–146, 148, 149, 151, 153, 155, 156

FSC
www.fsc.org
MIX
Papier | Fördert
gute Waldnutzung
FSC® C083411

Kolibri 360 GmbH
Ferdinand-Jühlke-Straße 7
99095 Erfurt, Deutschland
produktsicherheit@kolibri360.de